AF688085

# COGNITIVE THEORY OF DEPRESSION

## A GUIDE TO BECKIAN PSYCHOLOGY

# TABLE OF CONTENTS

# INTRODUCTION TO COGNITIVE THEORY OF DEPRESSION

## Theoretical Foundations

In delving into the theoretical foundations of cognitive theory in depression, it is imperative to acknowledge the seminal work of Dr. Aaron Beck, whose contributions have significantly shaped the landscape of psychological understanding and treatment modalities for depressive disorders. Beck's pioneering research and insights laid the groundwork for what has now become a cornerstone in the field of clinical psychology. The framework of cognitive theory revolves around the pivotal concept that our thoughts and beliefs about ourselves, the world, and the future influence our emotions and behaviors. This cognitive triad, consisting of personal views on oneself, the environment, and the future, forms the bedrock of Beck's theoretical paradigm. With an emphasis on the interplay between cognition, emotion, and behavior, the theory posits that distorted, negative thought patterns give rise to maladaptive emotional experiences and dysfunctional actions, thereby perpetuating the cycle of depression. By comprehensively exploring the cognitive underpinnings of depressive symptomatology, this approach provides crucial insights into the mechanisms underlying the onset and maintenance of depressive states. Furthermore, the theoretical foundations encompass a thorough analysis of automatic thoughts, which are spontaneous cognitions that often reflect a biased and distorted perception of reality. These automatic thoughts, frequently occurring in response to certain triggers or situations, have been identified as key determinants in shaping individuals' affective responses and behavioral patterns. Central to the theory is the notion that these cognitive distortions, such as personalization, overgeneralization, and catastrophic thinking, exert a profound influence on the individual's emotional well-being. Additionally, the cognitive model postulates the existence of underlying core beliefs or schemas, which are deeply ingrained, enduring cognitive structures representing one's fundamental beliefs about the self, the world, and the future. These core beliefs, predominantly developed during formative years, contribute to the formulation of recurring cognitive themes, influencing individuals' perceptions and interpretations of their experiences. Moreover, the theory elucidates the role of cognitive biases, elucidating how individuals selectively attend to, interpret, and recall information in a manner that aligns with their existing cognitive frameworks. These biases serve to reinforce negative cognitions, perpetuating the cycle of depressive symptoms. By integrating empirical findings and clinical observations, the theoretical foundations of cognitive theory provide a comprehensive understanding of the complex interplay between cognition, emotion, and behavior in the context of depression, offering invaluable insights into the nature of depressive disorders and paving the way for targeted interventions and therapeutic strategies.

**Principles of Cognitive Theory**

Cognitive theory posits several fundamental principles that underpin its approach to understanding and treating depression. At its core, the theory emphasizes the pivotal role of cognition in shaping emotions and behaviors, viewing mental health through the lens of cognitive processes. One key principle is the concept of automatic thoughts, where individuals experience rapid, uncontrolled cognitions that directly influence their mood and perception of events. These automatic thoughts often exhibit cognitive distortions, such as all-or-nothing thinking, overgeneralization, or personalization, which contribute to the maintenance of depressive symptoms.

Additionally, cognitive theory highlights the significance of underlying core beliefs or schemas, which serve as cognitive frameworks influencing how individuals interpret and respond to their experiences. These core beliefs are typically developed early in life and can become rigid, guiding individuals' perceptions of themselves, others, and the world. They often form the basis for recurrent negative thinking patterns observed in depression. Moreover, the theory underscores the influence of cognitive biases, wherein individuals selectively attend to information that aligns with their negative beliefs while disregarding or dismissing contrary evidence.

The principle of cognitive behavioral conceptualization is central to cognitive theory, emphasizing the formulation of individualized case conceptualizations that identify the specific cognitive patterns and mechanisms maintaining an individual's depressive symptoms. This thorough assessment guides the subsequent application of targeted cognitive interventions to modify maladaptive cognitive processes and foster more adaptive thinking patterns. The theory also recognizes the role of coping strategies and problem-solving skills in managing cognitive and emotional challenges.

Cognitive theory proposes the concept of learned helplessness, elucidating how ongoing negative experiences can lead individuals to perceive a lack of control over their circumstances, contributing to feelings of hopelessness and exacerbating depressive symptoms. Furthermore, the theory elucidates the role of rumination, a process wherein individuals repetitively dwell on negative thoughts and emotions, perpetuating the cycle of depression.

Cognitive theory's emphasis on collaboration between therapist and client and its structured, goal-oriented nature distinguish it as an effective therapeutic framework for depression. By integrating these principles into clinical practice, cognitive therapists aim to facilitate meaningful shifts in clients' cognitive processing and emotional well-being, ultimately alleviating distress and promoting long-term resilience.

### Significance in Mental Health

By emphasizing the role of thoughts, beliefs, and interpretations in shaping emotional experiences, cognitive theory offers valuable insights into the mechanisms underlying depressive symptoms. This understanding is crucial for mental health professionals, as it informs the development of targeted interventions that address the specific cognitive processes contributing to depressive states.

The application of cognitive theory in mental health extends beyond individual treatment to encompass broader societal implications. By recognizing the impact of cognitive distortions and maladaptive schemas on individuals' well-being, mental health practitioners can contribute to efforts aimed at promoting psychological resilience and preventing the onset of depressive disorders. Through education and awareness, the integration of cognitive principles into mental health discourse holds the potential to empower individuals in recognizing and challenging negative thought patterns, thereby fostering a more mentally healthy society.

The significance of cognitive theory in mental health is underscored by its compatibility with evidence-based practices and interventions. The empirical support for cognitive-behavioral approaches in addressing depression affirms the relevance of cognitive theory in guiding clinical decision-making and treatment planning. This alignment with research findings enhances the credibility and effectiveness of interventions, ultimately benefiting individuals grappling with depression.

In addition, the prominence of cognitive theory in mental health underscores its utility in multidisciplinary settings. Its adaptability and applicability across diverse therapeutic modalities enable collaboration among professionals from different disciplines, leading to integrated and holistic care for individuals experiencing depression. This interdisciplinary approach promotes comprehensive assessments and interventions that consider the cognitive dimensions of depression alongside biological, social, and environmental factors, thereby optimizing treatment outcomes.

Ultimately, the significance of cognitive theory in mental health lies in its capacity to engender hope and empowerment. By elucidating the modifiability of cognitive patterns and the potential for cognitive restructuring, this theoretical framework offers a message of optimism for individuals managing the complexities of depression. Through targeted interventions informed by cognitive theory, mental health professionals can guide individuals towards reclaiming agency over their thought processes and emotions, fostering a sense of control and progress on the path to recovery.

**Key Components of the Theory**

In the cognitive theory of depression, several key components contribute to the understanding of how individuals develop and experience depressive symptoms. Firstly, automatic thoughts play a crucial role in this theory. These are repetitive, spontaneous thought patterns that arise in response to particular situations or triggers, often influencing emotions and behaviors. Automatic thoughts can be negative, self-critical, or pessimistic, and they frequently contribute to distorted perceptions of reality.

Another essential component is cognitive distortions. According to the theory, individuals suffering from depression commonly experience one or more cognitive distortions, including overgeneralization, catastrophizing, magnification, and personalization. These distortions lead individuals to perceive events in a skewed and often exaggerated manner, perpetuating feelings of sadness, hopelessness, and despair.

Core beliefs and schemas also form fundamental components of the cognitive theory of depression. Core beliefs are deeply entrenched, fundamental beliefs about oneself, others, and the world, while schemas are cognitive frameworks that organize and interpret information. In the context of depression, maladaptive core beliefs and negative schemas can significantly influence an individual's perception of themselves, their experiences, and their future, thereby contributing to the maintenance of depressive symptoms.

The theory highlights the significance of cognitive triad, which consists of negative views regarding oneself, the world, and the future. This triad reflects the pervasive negative thinking patterns that characterize depression, leading individuals to have a bleak outlook on life and a diminished sense of self-worth.

Additionally, the cognitive theory emphasizes the role of cognitive processes in emotional regulation. Specifically, it proposes that dysfunctional cognitive processes result in heightened emotional reactivity and reduced ability to effectively manage negative emotions. This imbalance in emotional processing contributes to the perpetuation of depressive symptoms and the development of maladaptive coping strategies.

Lastly, the theory incorporates the concept of cognitive restructuring as a key component. Cognitive restructuring involves identifying and challenging maladaptive thought patterns and replacing them with more adaptive, realistic alternatives. Through targeted interventions aimed at modifying automatic thoughts, cognitive distortions, core beliefs, and cognitive triad, cognitive restructuring forms a cornerstone of cognitive therapy for depression, facilitating positive change in individuals' cognitive and emotional experiences.

**Interplay with Emotional Processes**

The interplay between cognitive theory of depression and emotional processes is a fundamental aspect that underpins the understanding of depressive disorders. It is well-established that emotions play a significant role in shaping an individual's cognitive experiences, and conversely, cognitive processes influence the regulation and manifestation of emotions. In the context of depression, this complex relationship becomes even more pronounced, as individuals often grapple with distorted perceptions and interpretations of their emotional states.

At the core of the interplay with emotional processes lies the concept of cognitive biases, which exert a profound influence on how individuals perceive and react to their emotions. Cognitive distortions, such as overgeneralization, magnification, and selective abstraction, can significantly impact the interpretation of emotional cues, leading to heightened sensitivity to negative affect and reduced capacity to effectively regulate one's mood. These biases contribute to the perpetuation of depressive symptoms by reinforcing maladaptive patterns of thinking and amplifying emotional distress.

The role of core beliefs and schemas in the processing of emotions cannot be understated. Depressive individuals often possess deeply ingrained negative schemas about themselves, others, and the world, which color their emotional experiences and contribute to the maintenance of their depressive state. For instance, an individual harboring beliefs of worthlessness may consistently interpret neutral or positive events through a lens of inadequacy, resulting in a persistent experience of sadness and hopelessness. The emotional resonance of these negative schemas perpetuates a cycle of negative emotions and reinforces the cognitive distortions that characterize depression.

The cognitive model emphasizes the influence of automatic thoughts on emotional reactivity, whereby dysfunctional thought patterns trigger intense emotional responses. When individuals engage in rumination, self-criticism, or catastrophic thinking, they fuel a cycle of escalating negative emotions, further entrenching the experience of depression. Additionally, the failure to challenge or restructure these automatic thoughts perpetuates maladaptive emotional responses, thereby prolonging the individual's experience of distress.

Understanding the interplay between cognitive processes and emotional functioning is pivotal for devising effective interventions and treatments for depression. By delineating the mechanisms through which cognition shapes emotional experiences, clinicians and researchers can develop targeted strategies to address and alleviate the emotional burden of depression.

## Comparison with Other Psychological Theories

Cognitive Theory of Depression has had a profound impact on the field of psychology, particularly in its approach to understanding and treating depressive disorders. A significant aspect of evaluating cognitive theory is to consider it in the context of other psychological theories that also aim to elucidate the nature of depression and related mental health conditions. This comparative analysis allows for a deeper understanding of the strengths and limitations inherent in each theoretical framework.

One prominent comparison can be made with the psychodynamic theory, which posits that unconscious conflicts and early life experiences heavily influence an individual's emotional well-being and behavior. While the emphasis on unconscious processes is a key divergence from cognitive theory, both approaches recognize the relevance of internal cognitive processes in shaping emotional experiences. However, cognitive theory differs in its focus on identifiable and modifiable thought patterns, presenting a more tangible target for therapeutic intervention compared to the abstract constructs of psychodynamic theory.

Another notable contrast exists when juxtaposing cognitive theory with behavioral theory. Behavioral theory emphasizes the role of external stimuli and learning experiences in determining behavior and emotions. Cognitive theory, on the other hand, highlights the central role of cognitive processes, such as perceptions, attributions, and beliefs, in driving emotional responses and behavior. It also acknowledges the individual's interpretation of events rather than solely focusing on observable behaviors. Nonetheless, contemporary therapies often integrate elements of both cognitive and behavioral techniques, acknowledging the value of addressing both internal cognitive processes and external behavioral responses.

Cognitive theory diverges from biological theories of depression, which underscore the neurochemical and neurological underpinnings of mental health disorders. While these perspectives offer valuable insights into the physiological aspects of depression, cognitive theory complements this by recognizing the interplay between biological factors and cognitive processes, shedding light on how an individual's cognitions and interpretations influence their lived experience of depression.

## Implications for Treatment

Based on the premise that distorted thoughts and maladaptive cognitive patterns contribute to the onset and maintenance of depressive symptoms, cognitive therapy has emerged as a prominent approach in treating depression. By targeting the negative thought processes, irrational beliefs, and dysfunctional schema that underpin depressive episodes, this therapeutic model offers practical implications for clinical interventions. One key aspect of treatment involves cognitive restructuring, which aims to identify and challenge the irrational and negative thought patterns characteristic of depression. Through techniques such as cognitive reframing, patients are encouraged to re-evaluate their automatic thoughts and adopt more balanced and constructive thinking patterns, thereby reducing the severity of depressive symptoms. Moreover, the emphasis on identifying and modifying cognitive distortions enables therapists to equip individuals with adaptive coping skills and resilience against future relapses. Furthermore, cognitive therapy emphasizes collaborative empiricism, wherein therapists work with clients to gather evidence that challenges their negative interpretations and beliefs. This systematic approach not only empowers individuals to actively engage in their own recovery but also fosters a sense of self-efficacy and agency in managing their mental health. The tailored nature of cognitive therapy allows for personalized treatment plans that address individual cognitive vulnerabilities, thus enhancing the efficacy of interventions. Additionally, the integration of behavioral activation techniques within cognitive therapy serves to counteract the withdrawal and avoidance behaviors commonly associated with depression, thereby promoting engagement in meaningful activities and reinforcing positive experiences. The transdiagnostic nature of cognitive theories also lends itself to addressing comorbid conditions and complex presentations often observed in clinical settings, presenting a holistic approach to treatment. As a result, the tangible and versatile applications of cognitive theory in the domain of treatment underscore its relevance and efficacy in clinical practice.

### Common Misconceptions and Clarifications

Common misconceptions about cognitive theory of depression often arise due to misunderstandings of its fundamental principles. One prevalent misunderstanding is the oversimplification of cognitive theory as merely a focus on 'positive thinking' or 'changing one's mindset.' In reality, cognitive theory entails a much more nuanced examination of thought patterns, core beliefs, and cognitive distortions that contribute to the development and maintenance of depressive symptoms. It is crucial to clarify that cognitive therapy does not minimize the impact of external factors such as trauma, socioeconomic conditions, or neurological predispositions on depression, but rather recognizes the reciprocal relationship between these external influences and internal cognitive processes. Another misconception is the belief that cognitive therapy places sole responsibility for one's depression on their thoughts, disregarding the multitude of contributing factors. However, cognitive theory acknowledges the multifaceted nature of depression, incorporating environmental, genetic, and neurobiological factors into its framework.

There is a common misconception that cognitive therapy dismisses the importance of emotions in the experience of depression. In fact, cognitive theory emphasizes the interplay between cognitions and emotions, highlighting how maladaptive thought patterns can influence emotional states and vice versa. It is important to understand that cognitive therapy does not seek to invalidate or suppress emotions, but rather aims to modify dysfunctional thought processes that perpetuate negative emotional experiences. Additionally, some may misinterpret cognitive therapy as an overly simplistic approach that ignores cultural and societal influences on mental health. In contrast, cognitive theory encourages clinicians to acknowledge cultural diversity and social dynamics in understanding and addressing depression, recognizing that individual experiences are shaped by broader contextual factors.

Addressing these misconceptions is critical in promoting a more accurate understanding of cognitive theory and its applications in the treatment of depression. By clarifying these misconceptions, both clinicians and individuals seeking therapy can better appreciate the comprehensive and integrative nature of cognitive therapy. In doing so, we can foster more effective therapeutic interventions and reduce stigma surrounding the utilization of cognitive approaches in mental health care.

# HISTORICAL CONTEXT AND DEVELOPMENT BY AARON BECK

## Origins of Cognitive Concepts in Psychiatry

The origins of cognitive concepts in psychiatry can be traced back to the early 20th century when influential thinkers such as Sigmund Freud and Carl Jung began exploring the relationship between thought patterns and emotional well-being. While traditional psychoanalytic theories emphasized the role of unconscious drives and early childhood experiences, a parallel stream of thought was emerging that sought to understand the impact of conscious cognitive processes on mental health.

One of the key influencers during this period was Otto Rank, whose work on the role of self-perception and the significance of individual will in shaping emotions laid the groundwork for the eventual integration of cognitive concepts into psychiatric discourse. Rank's emphasis on the subjective interpretation of experiences and the influence of personal narratives on emotional states provided an early glimpse into the potential relevance of cognitive frameworks within the field of psychiatry.

Additionally, the existentialist movement, with luminaries such as Viktor Frankl and Rollo May, underscored the existential dilemmas faced by individuals and highlighted the importance of subjective meaning-making in managing psychological distress. The existentialist perspective further accentuated the interactive nature of cognition and emotions, setting the stage for the gradual incorporation of cognitive concepts into the domain of psychiatric research and practice.

As the field evolved, the works of influential psychologists such as Jean Piaget and Lev Vygotsky brought forth developmental theories that illuminated the progressive nature of cognitive maturation and its impact on emotional regulation. Their perspectives not only emphasized the dynamic interplay between cognitive growth and emotional resilience but also paved the way for examining how maladaptive cognitive patterns could intersect with emotional disorders.

The rise of behaviorism, particularly the work of B.F. Skinner and John B. Watson, catapulted the study of observable behaviors into the forefront of psychological inquiry. However, it also sparked a juxtaposing quest to delve deeper into the internal cognitive mechanisms that mediated between stimuli and responses. This burgeoning interest in the 'black box' of the mind prompted researchers to unravel the cognitive underpinnings of emotional disturbances and marked a crucial juncture in the journey towards integrating cognitive concepts into psychiatric considerations.

### Aaron Beck's Early Contributions to Psychology

Aaron Temkin Beck, born in Providence, Rhode Island, in 1921, made profound early contributions to the field of psychology, particularly in the area of cognitive theory and therapy. After completing his medical studies at Yale University, Beck transitioned from a focus on psychoanalysis to pioneering a new approach that centered on understanding the cognitive underpinnings of emotional disturbance. Notably, during his tenure at the University of Pennsylvania, Beck began exploring the role of automatic thoughts in shaping emotions, which laid the groundwork for his influential theory of cognitive distortions. Through meticulous observation and clinical work, Beck discovered that individuals experiencing depression often exhibited a pattern of negative automatic thoughts, leading to the development of what would later be known as cognitive restructuring techniques in therapy. It was this revolutionary insight that catalyzed a paradigm shift in the conceptualization and treatment of psychological disorders. Beck's early contributions also extended into the domain of research methodologies, with his development of novel instruments to assess depression and anxiety proving instrumental in furthering empirical investigations. His seminal publication, "Cognitive Therapy and the Emotional Disorders," published in

1976, delineated his comprehensive model of cognitive therapy, providing a structured framework that effectively integrated theory and practice. Furthermore, Beck's endeavor to establish the Beck Institute for Cognitive Behavior Therapy has solidified his commitment to dissemination and training in cognitive therapy, ensuring that his influence endures beyond his own clinical and academic engagements. Beck's dedication to advancing the cognitive paradigm has undoubtedly reshaped the landscape of psychological theory and treatment, positioning him as a trailblazer whose early contributions continue to reverberate throughout contemporary psychology.

### The Evolution from Psychoanalysis to Cognitive Theory

In the mid-20th century, the predominance of psychoanalytic thinking in psychology and psychiatry set the stage for a significant paradigm shift. Aaron Beck's pivotal shift from psychoanalysis to cognitive theory marked a monumental evolution in the understanding and treatment of mental health disorders. This transformation was fueled by a growing dissatisfaction with the limitations of traditional psychoanalytic approaches, which heavily emphasized subconscious processes and early childhood experiences as primary determinants of psychological distress. Beck's departure from this prevailing Freudian perspective stemmed from his observations that patients often displayed immediate and pervasive thought distortions that seemed incongruent with the protracted explorations of deep-seated traumas advocated by psychoanalysis. Beck's divergence from conventional wisdom represented not only a bold departure but also a critical inflection point in the field of psychology.

Beck's blossoming ideas were further cultivated through his work with depressed patients. As he delved into the intricacies of their thought processes, Beck unearthed an array of cognitive patterns and distorted beliefs that manifested as key factors in their emotional suffering. This empirical grounding drove him to conceptualize depression as a disorder rooted in maladaptive thinking rather than repressed emotions or unresolved conflicts—a groundbreaking departure from the prevailing psychoanalytic orthodoxy. Additionally, Beck's parallel observation that clients actively participated in maintaining their depressive states through negative self-talk and cognitive biases challenged the passive patient role typically assigned in traditional psychoanalytic frameworks. These realizations laid the foundation for what would ultimately become the cognitive theory of depression—ushering in a pioneering approach that would revolutionize the field.

The transition from psychoanalysis to cognitive theory represented more than just a theoretical departure; it signaled a seismic shift in the therapeutic landscape. As traditional methods faced increasing scrutiny and criticism, Beck's radical reconceptualization opened doors to new avenues of understanding and treating psychological disorders. By refocusing attention on observable thoughts and behavior, the cognitive theory provided a refreshing departure from the conjectural and often impenetrable nature of psychoanalytic interpretations. Moreover, this transition implicated a fundamental reorientation of clinical practice, emphasizing the necessity for tangible interventions targeting identifiable cognitive distortions and automatic thoughts—an approach that eventually coalesced into the empirically supported framework of cognitive therapy. Through this shift, the once-dominant prominence of psychoanalytic theory began to wane, paving the way for a more rigorous, evidence-based approach that would come to define modern psychological intervention.

### Pioneering Research and Clinical Observations

During the formative years of Aaron Beck's work, his focus on the cognitive processes underlying emotional disorders led to groundbreaking research and clinical observations that reshaped the landscape of psychological theory and therapeutic practice. Through meticulous case studies and empirical investigations, Beck began to elucidate the interplay between thought patterns, emotional states, and behavioral responses in individuals experiencing depression. His pioneering research not only provided a new lens through which to understand mental health but also offered actionable insights for intervention and treatment. By meticulously documenting the cognitive distortions and dysfunctional beliefs prevalent in his patients, Beck revolutionized the approach to psychiatric assessment and proposed targeted strategies to address maladaptive cognitive schemas. Moreover, his emphasis on collaborative empiricism allowed for the integration of patients' perspectives and experiences into the therapeutic process, laying the groundwork for what would later become known as cognitive therapy. Beck's seminal clinical observations not only unveiled the cognitive underpinnings of depressive disorders but also paved the way for the systematic development of evidence-based interventions, setting a new standard for rigorous and effective psychological treatments. Furthermore, his holistic approach to understanding the interconnectedness of cognition, affect, and behavior sparked a paradigm shift in the field, prompting a departure from traditional symptom-focused models to a more comprehensive understanding of psychological distress. The meticulous documentation of his clinical insights, coupled with the advancement of rigorous research methodologies, established a solid empirical foundation for the cognitive theory of depression. Thus, Beck's pioneering research and clinical observations laid the cornerstone for a transformative shift in the conceptualization and treatment of depression, shaping the course of modern mental health practice.

### Initial Resistances and Paradigm Shifts

In the early days, Aaron Beck's cognitive theory faced significant resistance and skepticism from within the psychological community. The prevailing influence of psychoanalysis and behaviorism during the mid-20th century posed considerable hurdles for the acceptance of a new paradigm. Beck's departure from the dominant psychoanalytic tradition, by emphasizing conscious thoughts and beliefs over unconscious drives, encountered substantial opposition, with many viewing his ideas as overly reductionist and simplistic. Additionally, the behavioral camp questioned the efficacy and relevance of cognition in understanding and treating mental disorders. This resistance to acknowledging cognitive processes as pivotal in shaping emotional experiences led to numerous debates and challenges to the very foundation of Beck's theory. However, Beck's unwavering commitment to empirical evidence gradually initiated a transformative paradigm shift within the field of psychology. Through rigorous research and systematic clinical observations, Beck demonstrated that cognitive distortions and dysfunctional thought patterns significantly contributed to the development and maintenance of depression and other mood disorders. This groundbreaking evidence not only challenged the existing paradigms but also laid the groundwork for a new era in the understanding and treatment of psychological ailments. As a result of these paradigm shifts, cognitive therapy emerged as a legitimate and impactful approach, gaining traction among practitioners and researchers alike.

### Influential Publications and Their Impact

The evolution of cognitive theory, as espoused by Aaron Beck, has been notably shaped by a series of influential publications that not only elucidated the theoretical framework but also galvanized a paradigm shift within the psychological community. Beck's seminal works, including 'Cognitive Therapy and the Emotional Disorders' and 'Cognitive Therapy of Depression', provided a comprehensive delineation of the cognitive model of psychopathology, outlining its core tenets and therapeutic applications. These publications served as pivotal catalysts in disseminating cognitive theory to the broader academic and clinical milieu.

The impact of these publications extended beyond mere theoretical elucidation; they spurred an empirical movement by inspiring research endeavors aiming to validate and refine cognitive principles. Beck's rigorous empirical approach laid the groundwork for subsequent studies that substantiated the efficacy of cognitive interventions in ameliorating depressive symptoms, thereby solidifying the theory's standing within the spheres of evidence-based practice.

The assimilation of cognitive theory into the fabric of psychological discourse was propelled by the lucid and accessible nature of Beck's publications, which facilitated the seamless integration of cognitive concepts into existing psychotherapeutic frameworks. This accessibility democratized the dissemination of cognitive principles and rendered them applicable to a wide array of clinical contexts, fostering a comprehensive understanding of the role of distorted cognition in affecting emotional states.

Notably, these publications did not only resonate within the confines of academia; they reverberated across clinical settings, engendering a transformative outlook on the conceptualization and treatment of various psychiatric disorders. By elucidating the interplay between cognition and affect, Beck's publications offered a path-breaking departure from traditional psychodynamic perspectives, stimulating a renaissance in therapeutic approaches that centered on cognitive restructuring and the cultivation of adaptive coping mechanisms.

Ultimately, the impact of Beck's influential publications lies in their role as a linchpin for the propagation and validation of cognitive theory, perpetuating its ascent to a preeminent position within contemporary psychological discourse.

### Integration with Existing Psychological Theories

As cognitive theory continued to gain prominence in the field of psychology, its integration with existing psychological theories became a subject of significant academic and clinical interest. The synthesis of cognitive concepts with established theoretical frameworks such as behaviorism, psychoanalysis, and humanistic psychology brought about a paradigmatic shift in the understanding and treatment of mental health disorders.

One of the key areas of integration was with behaviorism, which traditionally focused on observable behaviors and external stimuli. Aaron Beck's cognitive theory facilitated a nuanced exploration of the internal cognitive processes underlying these behaviors, thereby enriching the understanding of psychological phenomena beyond surface-level observations. This integration led to the development of cognitive behavioral approaches that have demonstrated efficacy in addressing a wide range of psychological disorders.

The integration with psychoanalytic perspectives, which emphasized unconscious motivations and early life experiences, provided a complementary dimension to cognitive theory. By acknowledging the influence of past experiences and the role of unconscious cognitive structures, cognitive theorists expanded the conceptualization of human cognition and emotion. This integration offered a holistic framework for understanding the complex interplay between conscious and unconscious mental processes in shaping an individual's psychological well-being.

The incorporation of humanistic psychology's emphasis on personal growth, self-actualization, and subjective experience also enriched cognitive theory by highlighting the significance of meaning-making and existential concerns in the context of depression and other psychopathologies. This integration encouraged a broader perspective that encompassed both cognitive distortions and subjective interpretations of experiences, underscoring the multifaceted nature of psychological distress.

The amalgamation of cognitive theory with neurobiological models contributed to a more comprehensive understanding of the neural underpinnings of cognitive processes and emotional regulation. Advances in neuroscience have elucidated the connections between cognitive functions, emotional states, and neurophysiological mechanisms, providing empirical support for the interconnectedness of cognitive and biological factors in mental health.

In essence, the integration of cognitive theory with various established psychological frameworks not only broadened the scope of theoretical understanding but also enhanced the versatility of therapeutic interventions. Cognitive therapists could draw from diverse psychological traditions to tailor interventions that address the cognitive, emotional, behavioral, and existential dimensions of depression and related conditions, thereby fostering a more holistic approach to mental health care.

**Beck's Foundational Experiments and Findings**

Aaron Beck's pioneering experiments and findings have left an indelible mark on the understanding and treatment of psychological disorders. One of Beck's foundational contributions was his investigation into the phenomenon of cognitive distortions, which are erroneous thought patterns that contribute to the maintenance of depressive symptoms. Through rigorous empirical inquiry, Beck systematically identified and categorized common cognitive distortions such as overgeneralization, catastrophizing, and selective abstraction. These experiments not only provided empirical support for his cognitive theory of depression but also laid the groundwork for the development of cognitive restructuring techniques in therapy. Additionally, Beck's research delved into the concept of automatic thoughts, revealing their pervasive nature in influencing emotional states and behavior. Through meticulous observation and controlled studies, Beck illuminated the interplay between automatic thoughts and the perpetuation of depressive cycles. Moreover, his investigations underscored the discriminatory nature of these automatic thoughts, shedding light on how individuals with depression tend to selectively attend to negative stimuli while dismissing positive or neutral experiences. This comprehensive understanding of automatic thoughts became instrumental in the formulation of cognitive interventions aimed at challenging and modifying dysfunctional thought patterns. Beck's findings in the areas of cognitive triad and schema theory further solidified the empirical foundation of cognitive therapy. By elucidating the triangulated relationship between one's view of self, the world, and the future, Beck offered valuable insights into the cognitive underpinnings of depression. Furthermore, his exploration of maladaptive schemas unveiled the influence of early experiences on shaping core beliefs and cognitive processing. Beck's empirical observations and experimental studies not only propelled the refinement of cognitive therapy techniques but also enriched the broader landscape of psychotherapy.

### Contributions to the Broader Field of Psychotherapy

Aaron Beck's impact on the broader field of psychotherapy is profound and far-reaching, extending beyond the boundaries of his cognitive theory of depression. His innovative approach to understanding and treating mental health disorders has revolutionized the practice of psychotherapy, significantly influencing a wide range of therapeutic modalities and treatment protocols.

One of Beck's most significant contributions lies in his emphasis on collaboration and active engagement between the therapist and the client. By promoting a transparent and participatory dynamic during therapy sessions, Beck shifted the traditional power dynamics within the therapeutic relationship, empowering clients to take an active role in their own healing process. This shift has had a lasting impact on various therapeutic approaches, promoting a more egalitarian and client-centered model of care across the psychotherapeutic landscape.

Beck's development of structured, time-limited therapy protocols set a new standard for efficiency and effectiveness in psychotherapeutic interventions. By introducing systematic and goal-oriented frameworks for addressing specific mental health concerns, Beck not only enhanced the accountability and measurability of therapeutic outcomes but also paved the way for the development of evidence-based practices within psychotherapy. The influence of these innovations extends to diverse therapeutic orientations, inspiring the integration of structured and time-limited elements into various psychotherapeutic modalities.

Additionally, Beck's introduction of cognitive restructuring techniques, aimed at identifying and challenging maladaptive thought patterns, has been instrumental in shaping the landscape of contemporary psychotherapy. These techniques have transcended the confines of cognitive therapy and are now widely incorporated into different therapeutic approaches, contributing to a more comprehensive and holistic understanding of the interplay between cognition, emotion, and behavior in mental health treatment.

Beck's clarifications on the role of automatic thoughts and cognitive distortions have provided invaluable insights into the nature of psychological suffering, offering a common framework for understanding and addressing a wide array of emotional and behavioral disturbances across diverse clinical populations. As a result, these conceptual advancements have permeated the fabric of psychotherapeutic education and practice, enriching the theoretical underpinnings and practical applications of numerous therapeutic modalities.

### Legacy of Aaron Beck in Contemporary Psychology

One of the most significant aspects of Beck's legacy lies in the widespread integration of cognitive therapy techniques across diverse modalities of psychological treatment. His emphasis on identifying and modifying maladaptive thought patterns has informed not only dedicated cognitive therapy sessions but also broader therapeutic interventions, such as dialectical behavior therapy (DBT) and acceptance and commitment therapy (ACT). The foundational principles of cognitive restructuring and collaborative empiricism developed by Beck have become ubiquitous, permeating the fabric of contemporary psychological practice.

Beck's legacy is evident in the continuous refinement and expansion of cognitive-based interventions. From the development of transdiagnostic approaches to the application of cognitive principles in novel contexts such as digital mental health interventions, Beck's influence endures through ongoing advancements that build upon his original concepts. Researchers and clinicians alike have embraced and adapted Beck's framework to address a wide array of psychological conditions, ensuring its relevance and efficacy in modern clinical settings.

Beyond specific therapeutic techniques, Beck's legacy extends to the broader conceptualization of psychopathology and human cognition. His early insights into the role of cognitive distortions and negative schemas in perpetuating emotional distress have catalyzed paradigm shifts in understanding and treating various mental health disorders. Through his holistic approach, integrating cognitive, emotional, and behavioral components, Beck laid the groundwork for a more comprehensive and nuanced comprehension of the interplay between psychological processes.

Beck's legacy reverberates through the training and education of future mental health professionals. The incorporation of cognitive theory into graduate programs, continuing education initiatives, and clinical supervision underscores the relevance of his contributions. Clinicians across diverse disciplines benefit from Beck's intellectual bequest, equipping them with invaluable tools to manage the complexities of human experience and alleviate individual suffering.

# KEY POSTULATES AND CONCEPTS

## Automatic Thoughts in Depression

1. Definition and Characteristics:

Automatic thoughts, a cornerstone of cognitive theory in depression, are the rapid and involuntary cognitions that occur in response to specific situations or stimuli. These thoughts are often brief, frequent, and highly accessible, manifesting as an individual's immediate interpretation of events or experiences without deliberate rationalization. Their defining characteristics underscore their impulsive nature, lacking the conscious reasoning associated with reflective thinking. These cognitions are typically undetected by the individual, embedding themselves seamlessly into the fabric of consciousness. Moreover, automatic thoughts are predominantly negative and distorted in nature, contributing significantly to the maintenance and exacerbation of depressive symptoms. As pivotal components of cognitive distortions, these thoughts fuel maladaptive schemas and perpetuate emotional distress. The identification and elucidation of automatic thoughts provide crucial insights into the cognitive processes underlying depression, shedding light on the interplay between cognition, emotion, and behavior. Understanding the defining features of automatic thoughts is imperative in formulating targeted therapeutic interventions aimed at alleviating distress and promoting cognitive restructuring.

2. The Role of Automatic Thoughts in Emotional Responses:

Automatic thoughts play a crucial role in shaping emotional responses among individuals experiencing depressive disorders. As individuals manage their daily experiences, automatic thoughts arise seamlessly and influence the emotional landscape by triggering feelings of sadness, hopelessness, or despair. Understanding the connection between automatic thoughts and emotional responses is pivotal in comprehending the depth of depressive cognition. The immediacy and intensity of these thoughts can exacerbate negative affect and perpetuate cycles of distress. Moreover, the repetitive nature of automatic thoughts reinforces the corresponding emotions, creating a self-perpetuating cycle of negativity. It is essential to recognize that automatic thoughts not only impact emotional experiences but also contribute to the maintenance of depressive symptoms. These thoughts often distort reality and generate overwhelming feelings of worthlessness or failure, further intensifying emotional responses. Additionally, the subconscious nature of automatic thoughts makes them challenging to identify and alter, amplifying their pervasive impact on emotional well-being. By recognizing the potency of automatic thoughts in shaping emotional responses, individuals and mental health professionals can delve deeper into understanding the complexities of depressive disorders and tailor interventions accordingly. Furthermore, by addressing the interplay between automatic thoughts and emotional responses, therapeutic approaches can target the core cognitive processes underlying depressive symptomatology, thereby fostering more effective treatment outcomes.

3. Origins and Development of Automatic Thoughts:

Automatic thoughts in depression are shaped by a complex interplay of factors related to an individual's cognitive processes, emotional experiences, and life events. The origins and development of these automatic thoughts can be traced back to various psychological mechanisms and environmental influences. One key factor contributing to the development of automatic thoughts is early childhood experiences, particularly those involving significant emotional or traumatic events. These experiences can form the basis for core beliefs and schemas that influence how individuals perceive themselves, others, and the world around them. Additionally, interpersonal relationships and attachment patterns play a crucial role in shaping automatic thoughts, as they contribute to the formation of cognitive structures and interpretive frameworks. Furthermore, ongoing stressors, societal pressures, and cultural factors can also impact the development of automatic thoughts, leading individuals to adopt specific cognitive patterns in response to their environment. Over time, repeated exposure to these influential factors can lead to the solidification of maladaptive cognitive processes, resulting in the emergence of persistent automatic thoughts commonly associated with depression. As automatic thoughts continue to develop and evolve throughout the lifespan, they become ingrained in an individual's cognitive repertoire, influencing their perceptions, emotions, and behaviors. Understanding the origins and development of automatic thoughts in depression is essential for clinicians and researchers seeking to address and intervene in cognitive processes underlying depressive disorders. By unraveling the complex pathways that give rise to automatic thoughts, professionals can gain valuable insights into the etiology of depressive cognition and tailor interventions to effectively target and modify these cognitive patterns.

4. Types of Automatic Thoughts Commonly Observed in Depression:

Automatic thoughts in depression are diverse and can manifest in various forms, impacting individuals' emotional well-being and daily functioning. Common types of automatic thoughts observed in depression encompass cognitive distortions such as arbitrary inference, overgeneralization, magnification or minimization, personalization, and selective abstraction. Arbitrary inference involves making conclusions without supporting evidence, often attributing negative interpretations to events or experiences without rational basis. Overgeneralization refers to drawing general conclusions based on limited instances, leading individuals to apply negative experiences to broad aspects of their lives. Magnification or minimization involves exaggerating the significance of negative events while diminishing positive occurrences, contributing to a distorted perception of reality. Personalization occurs when individuals attribute external events to themselves without valid reasons, assuming unnecessary responsibility for negative outcomes. Selective abstraction entails focusing solely on negative details while discounting positive aspects of a situation, reinforcing negative cognitive patterns. Additionally, catastrophic thinking, commonly observed in depression, involves envisioning the worst-case scenarios, amplifying fears and anxieties. These automatic thoughts denote the pervasive nature of depressive cognition and underscore the importance of identifying and addressing these cognitive distortions in therapeutic interventions.

5. Impact of Negative Automatic Thoughts on Daily Functioning:

Negative automatic thoughts, as a hallmark of depressive cognitive processing, exert profound influence on an individual's daily functioning across various domains. These pervasive cognitions can significantly impair an individual's ability to engage in adaptive behaviors, leading to disruptions in personal, social, and occupational spheres. In interpersonal relationships, the impact of negative automatic thoughts is palpable, as individuals may withdraw from social interactions or perceive benign cues as critical, thereby straining connections with others. Additionally, these individuals may exhibit hesitancy in seeking support, as their negative automatic thoughts fuel feelings of unworthiness and alienation.

The impact of negative automatic thoughts extends to occupational endeavors. Individuals gripped by such cognitions may experience diminished concentration, persistent self-doubt, and reduced motivation, which can impede their performance at work or hinder their pursuit of career advancement opportunities. In personal pursuits, negative automatic thoughts can manifest as excessive self-criticism and defeatist attitudes, sapping the individual's enthusiasm for hobbies or physical activities that once brought them joy.

Beyond its interpersonal and occupational consequences, the insidious influence of negative automatic thoughts on daily functioning permeates into the sphere of self-care and emotional regulation. Individuals immersed in negative automatic thoughts may struggle with maintaining healthy lifestyle practices, such as proper nutrition, regular exercise, and adequate sleep, as their distorted perceptions contribute to a sense of apathy and hopelessness. Moreover, these individuals face heightened vulnerability to emotional dysregulation, with negative automatic thoughts amplifying feelings of despair, anxiety, and helplessness, thereby exacerbating the burden of depression.

Understanding the far-reaching impact of negative automatic thoughts on daily functioning underscores the pressing need for effective interventions aimed at challenging and modifying these destructive cognitions. By addressing the interplay between thoughts, emotions, and behavior, clinicians can equip individuals with practical strategies to mitigate the deleterious effects of negative automatic thoughts, fostering an enhanced capacity for adaptive, resilient functioning amidst the challenges posed by depressive cognitive processes.

6. Cognitive Distortions Underlying Automatic Thoughts:

Automatic thoughts in depression are often driven by cognitive distortions that lead individuals to perceive reality in a biased and negative manner. These distortions, identified by Aaron Beck, play a crucial role in shaping automatic thoughts and subsequent emotional responses. One of the most common cognitive distortions is 'all-or-nothing thinking,' where individuals view situations in extreme black-and-white terms, leading to polarization of experiences into either entirely positive or negative outcomes. This distortion can contribute to the amplification of negative automatic thoughts, as any minor setback may be perceived as a complete failure.

Another prevalent distortion is 'catastrophizing,' which involves the exaggerated anticipation of disaster or worst-case scenarios. This cognitive distortion can intensify the impact of negative automatic thoughts, leading individuals to imagine the most severe consequences of a situation, thereby heightening their distress and anxiety levels. Additionally, 'mental filtering' represents a cognitive distortion through which individuals selectively focus on negative aspects of a situation while ignoring any positive elements. This selective attention to negativity reinforces the occurrence of negative automatic thoughts, further perpetuating the cycle of depression.

On the other hand, 'overgeneralization' is a cognitive distortion characterized by the tendency to draw broad, sweeping conclusions based on limited evidence or single incidents. In the context of automatic thoughts, overgeneralization can lead individuals to extrapolate negative experiences to all areas of their lives, fostering a pervasive sense of hopelessness and despair. Moreover, 'personalization' involves the tendency to attribute excessive responsibility to oneself for external events, leading to an overestimation of one's negative impact on situations. This cognitive distortion plays a significant role in generating self-blaming automatic thoughts, which contribute to feelings of guilt and inadequacy.

Lastly, 'emotional reasoning' represents a cognitive distortion wherein individuals interpret their emotions as reflective of objective reality, disregarding any evidence to the contrary. In the context of automatic thoughts, emotional reasoning can lead individuals to accept their negative emotions as proof of negative circumstances, reinforcing the validity of their negative automatic thoughts. Understanding these cognitive distortions is essential in addressing automatic thoughts within a cognitive framework, as it allows for targeted interventions aimed at challenging and modifying these distorted thinking patterns.

7. Negative Automatic Thoughts:

Automatic thoughts often reflect underlying cognitive distortions, such as overgeneralization, magnification, and personalization, which contribute to the maintenance of depressive symptoms. Clinicians employ various techniques to help individuals recognize and address these thought patterns.

The initial step in this process involves fostering awareness of automatic thoughts through self-monitoring and structured activities, such as thought records or journals. These tools enable individuals to track their thoughts, emotions, and associated situations, facilitating the identification of recurring negative thought patterns. Through systematic documentation, individuals can gain insight into the triggers and effects of their automatic thoughts, paving the way for subsequent intervention.

Once negative automatic thoughts are identified, clinicians guide individuals in evaluating the evidence for and against these thoughts. This process entails examining the accuracy and validity of their interpretations and considering alternative explanations for the triggering events. By encouraging a balanced exploration of the evidence, individuals can challenge the absoluteness of their negative thinking and develop more realistic perspectives.

Cognitive restructuring techniques are employed to modify entrenched negative thought patterns. Individuals are encouraged to reframe their automatic thoughts by substituting them with more adaptive, rational alternatives. This restructuring process involves stepping back from initial emotional reactions and engaging in deliberate cognitive reappraisal. Through repeated practice, individuals can cultivate a habit of critically evaluating their automatic thoughts and gradually adopting healthier cognitive habits.

To supplement these techniques, behavioral experiments are often utilized to test the validity of automatic thoughts in real-world contexts. Individuals are encouraged to engage in behavior that challenges their negative beliefs or expectations, providing opportunities to gather concrete evidence that contradicts their automatic thoughts. This experiential approach helps individuals overcome avoidance behaviors and validates the potential mismatch between their predictions and actual outcomes, leading to cognitive shifts.

Mindfulness-based practices are integrated to enhance individuals' capacity to observe their automatic thoughts without immediate judgment or reactivity. Mindfulness facilitates the development of a non-reactive awareness of thought patterns, allowing individuals to detach from their automatic thoughts and optimize their response flexibility. By cultivating present-moment attention, individuals can foster a more accepting and compassionate stance toward their cognitive processes, reducing the emotional impact of negative automatic thoughts.

8. Clinical Techniques for Addressing Automatic Thoughts:

In addressing automatic thoughts within the therapeutic context, clinicians utilize a range of evidence-based techniques to assist individuals in challenging and modifying their cognitive processes. Cognitive Restructuring, a cornerstone method in cognitive therapy, involves identifying negative automatic thoughts, examining the underlying assumptions and cognitive distortions, and devising rational alternatives. By guiding individuals to systematically question the validity of their automatic thoughts, therapists aid in altering maladaptive thought patterns and fostering more adaptive thinking strategies.

Another pivotal clinical strategy is Behavioral Experiments, wherein individuals engage in experiential activities designed to test the validity of their automatic thoughts. Through collaborative efforts between the therapist and the individual, real-life situations are created to challenge the beliefs underpinning automatic thoughts. The outcomes of these experiments provide individuals with empirical evidence supporting the adaptability of their thoughts, instilling a sense of empowerment and fostering cognitive flexibility. Additionally, Imagery Rescripting, a technique often utilized in cases of traumatic automatic thoughts, involves revisiting distressing memories or images and reframing them to generate alternative, less distressing cognitive patterns.

Mindfulness-Based Interventions have gained prominence in addressing automatic thoughts by cultivating present-moment awareness and acceptance. Techniques such as mindfulness meditation encourage individuals to observe their thoughts without judgment, allowing them to develop a more balanced and non-reactive relationship with their cognitive processes. This heightened self-awareness enables individuals to disengage from automatic thoughts and choose more adaptive responses.

Metacognitive Strategies play a central role in treating automatic thoughts. By promoting metacognitive awareness, individuals learn to recognize recurring thought patterns and accompanying emotional and behavioral responses. Through metacognitive interventions, individuals acquire the skills to evaluate the efficiency of their thought processes and implement strategic modifications, thereby enhancing cognitive regulation and reducing reliance on automatic negative thinking.

Additionally, Group Therapy can be an effective platform for addressing automatic thoughts. Participating in a group setting provides individuals with opportunities for social support, perspective-taking, and shared experiences, contributing to the validation and normalization of their cognitive struggles. These therapeutic interactions foster an environment conducive to challenging and reconstructing automatic thoughts, facilitating the cultivation of new coping mechanisms and adaptive cognitive schemas.

Finally, Cognitive Behavioral Homework Assignments offer individuals structured tasks that reinforce learning and promote the application of cognitive techniques outside the therapeutic setting. By engaging in homework assignments that target automatic thoughts, individuals continue to practice and integrate the acquired cognitive strategies into their daily lives, further consolidating cognitive restructuring and fostering lasting change.

## 9. Research Findings Related to Automatic Thoughts in Depressive Disorders:

Over the years, numerous studies have contributed significantly to our understanding of the interplay between automatic thoughts and depressive symptoms. Through empirical investigations, researchers have unearthed compelling evidence regarding the pervasive nature of negative automatic thoughts in individuals grappling with depression. These findings underscore the profound impact of automatic thoughts on emotional experiences and cognitive processing, shedding light on their role as pivotal determinants of the depressive symptomatology.

One notable line of research has focused on the relationship between specific types of automatic thoughts and distinct subtypes of depressive disorders. By elucidating the nuanced manifestations of automatic thoughts across varying subgroups of individuals with depression, researchers have discerned valuable nuances that inform tailored interventions and targeted treatment approaches. Moreover, longitudinal studies have offered invaluable insights into the temporal dynamics of automatic thoughts, unveiling their fluctuating patterns and influence on the course of depressive illnesses.

Advancements in neuroimaging techniques have revolutionized our understanding of the neural substrates underpinning automatic thoughts in depression. Sophisticated neurobiological studies have illuminated the neurocognitive mechanisms implicated in the generation and modulation of automatic thoughts, unraveling the network of brain regions implicated in maladaptive cognitive processes. These neuroscientific revelations offer a comprehensive framework for comprehending the neural underpinnings of automatic thoughts, thus paving the way for innovative therapeutic interventions targeting these neural circuits.

Additionally, research efforts have delineated the differential efficacy of various therapeutic modalities in ameliorating automatic thoughts and associated depressive symptoms. Comparative clinical trials have provided empirical support for the effectiveness of cognitive restructuring techniques in modifying maladaptive automatic thoughts, highlighting the pivotal role of cognitive-behavioral interventions in mitigating the deleterious impact of negative automatic thoughts. Moreover, meta-analytic studies synthesizing data from a plethora of trials have furnished robust evidence substantiating the enduring benefits of addressing automatic thoughts within the context of comprehensive treatment protocols.

10. Integrating Insights into Therapeutic Practice:

The insights gleaned from research findings related to automatic thoughts in depressive disorders offer valuable implications for therapeutic practice. Integrating these insights into clinical interventions can significantly enhance the effectiveness of therapeutic approaches for individuals experiencing depression. By acknowledging the pervasive influence of automatic thoughts and their role in sustaining depressive symptoms, mental health professionals can tailor treatment strategies to address these cognitive patterns.

Central to the integration of insights into therapeutic practice is the emphasis on cognitive restructuring. This process involves identifying and challenging maladaptive automatic thoughts to facilitate a shift towards more adaptive and balanced thinking patterns. Therapists can employ various cognitive-behavioral techniques such as Socratic questioning, behavioral experiments, and examining evidence for and against automatic thoughts to accomplish this restructuring. Moreover, incorporating mindfulness-based interventions can further augment the effectiveness of addressing automatic thoughts by promoting present-moment awareness and reducing ruminative thinking.

Therapeutic modalities such as Acceptance and Commitment Therapy (ACT) and Dialectical Behavior Therapy (DBT) provide additional avenues for integrating insights related to automatic thoughts into clinical practice. ACT emphasizes acceptance of internal experiences, diffusion from cognitive fusion, and value-based living, enabling individuals to develop a more flexible relationship with their thoughts. On the other hand, DBT incorporates skills training in emotion regulation and distress tolerance, offering practical tools to manage the impact of automatic thoughts on emotional well-being.

It is crucial for mental health professionals to foster collaboration with clients when integrating insights into therapeutic practice. Establishing a collaborative and empathic therapeutic alliance creates a conducive environment for clients to explore and challenge their automatic thoughts without judgment. The collaborative nature of therapy empowers individuals to actively participate in the process of change and fosters a sense of agency in managing their cognitive patterns. Additionally, highlighting the interactive nature of cognitive and emotional processes can aid clients in recognizing the bidirectional influence between their thoughts and emotions, paving the way for deeper self-understanding and mastery over their cognitive responses.

In conclusion, integrating insights from research on automatic thoughts into therapeutic practice holds substantial promise in enhancing treatment outcomes for individuals grappling with depressive disorders. By implementing evidence-based interventions rooted in cognitive restructuring, mindfulness-based approaches, and specialized therapeutic modalities, mental health professionals can equip clients with the necessary tools to manage and modify their automatic thoughts. Furthermore, fostering a collaborative therapeutic relationship empowers individuals to take an active role in challenging and reshaping their cognitive patterns, ultimately contributing to a more holistic and effective approach to treating depression.

## The Cognitive Triad - Self, World, and Future

1. Historical Foundation and Theory Development:

The historical foundation and theory development of the cognitive triad in the context of depression represent a pivotal aspect of understanding the evolution of cognitive theories in psychology. The roots of the cognitive triad can be traced back to Aaron Beck, who introduced the concept as a central component of his cognitive theory of depression. Beck's pioneering research in the 1960s emphasized the fundamental role of distorted thinking patterns in the onset and perpetuation of depressive symptoms, laying the groundwork for the cognitive triad model. Beck postulated that individuals with depression tend to exhibit negative distortions in their perceptions of self, world, and future, forming the basis of the cognitive triad framework. Building on this foundation, subsequent scholars and researchers have expanded and refined the cognitive triad theory, contributing to its continued relevance in contemporary psychological discourse. The theoretical development of the cognitive triad represents a convergence of insights from cognitive psychology, clinical experience, and empirical investigations, culminating in a nuanced understanding of the interconnected cognitive processes underlying depressive states. Over time, this multifaceted approach has shaped the conceptualization and refinement of the triad, solidifying its significance as a core construct in the cognitive-behavioral model of depression. The iterative nature of theory development in cognitive psychology has led to the integration of diverse perspectives, drawing from fields such as social cognition, emotion regulation, and information processing. These interdisciplinary influences have enriched our comprehension of the cognitive triad, thereby enhancing its applicability to the complex nature of depressive disorders. As the cognitive triad continues to evolve, contemporary research endeavors have sought to elucidate its nuanced manifestations across diverse populations and cultural contexts. This ongoing exploration contributes to the continuous enrichment of the cognitive triad theory, fostering a more comprehensive framework for understanding the cognitive dimensions of depression and informing tailored interventions and treatment strategies.

2. Self-Perception Within the Triad:

Self-perception, within the cognitive triad framework, offers valuable insights into an individual's cognitive processes and emotional experiences. As individuals traverse their existence, they continuously construct and interpret the narrative of the 'self' within the context of their lives. The cognitive triad emphasizes that negative self-perceptions play a pivotal role in propagating and sustaining depressive states. By scrutinizing the self-perception element within the triad, we delve into the web of beliefs, attitudes, and evaluations that individuals hold about themselves. This analysis necessitates an exploration of core beliefs and their influence on the perception of the self. Moreover, it involves an examination of how individuals process and internalize feedback from their social environments, impacting their sense of worth and competence. These self-evaluations are not static but rather dynamic, shaped by past experiences, societal standards, and interpersonal dynamics. The intersection of these components contributes to the overarching self-perception, influencing cognitive processes and emotional well-being. Through this analysis, we unravel the interplay between self-esteem, self-concept, and the formation of maladaptive schemas. Furthermore, we shed light on the mechanisms through which negative self-perceptions manifest in daily activities, relationships, and overall functioning. Understanding the intricacies of self-perception within the triad is paramount in developing targeted interventions to ameliorate depression and enhance psychological well-being. By delineating the nuanced pathways through which negative self-perceptions contribute to depressive symptomatology, mental health professionals can devise tailored therapeutic approaches to challenge and restructure dysfunctional beliefs. Additionally, this analysis guides researchers in devising rigorous methodologies to empirically investigate the impact of self-perception on depressive cognition and emotion. Delving into the depths of self-perception within the cognitive triad paves the way for comprehensive comprehension of depression and fosters avenues for effective intervention strategies.

3. Cognitive Interpretation of the World - External Influences:

The cognitive interpretation of the world plays a pivotal role in shaping an individual's perception of reality, thereby significantly influencing their emotional and psychological well-being. At its core, the cognitive interpretation of the world is influenced by various external stimuli, including interpersonal interactions, societal norms, media portrayals, and situational experiences. These stimuli serve as the building blocks for constructing an individual's cognitive schema of the world, affecting their perceptions of safety, trust, and predictability. Moreover, societal and cultural factors play a significant role in shaping one's worldview, as they influence the attribution of meaning to events and experiences.

It is imperative to recognize the role of social comparison in the formation of cognitive interpretations. The tendency to compare oneself with others, especially in the age of ubiquitous social media, can give rise to distorted perceptions of success, happiness, and fulfillment. These comparisons often fuel negative self-evaluations and perpetuate maladaptive cognitive patterns, thereby contributing to the maintenance of depressive symptoms.

The portrayal of societal ideals and beauty standards in the media can significantly impact an individual's cognitive interpretation of their own worth and significance. Exposure to unrealistic and idealized images may distort one's perception of self-worth, attributing exaggerated importance to physical appearance and material possessions. Such skewed interpretations can lead to pervasive feelings of inadequacy and unworthiness, reinforcing negative cognitive biases.

In addition to individual-level influences, contextual factors, such as economic instability, political turmoil, and societal discrimination, can exert a profound impact on cognitive interpretations of the world. Economic hardships, for instance, can engender feelings of hopelessness and despair, amplifying negative cognitive appraisals of personal efficacy and control.

4. Comparative Overview of the Components of the Triad:

The cognitive triad encompasses three interconnected components: the self, the world, and the future. Each component plays a crucial role in shaping an individual's cognitive processes and overall mental well-being. The 'self' component involves one's perception of themselves, encompassing beliefs about personal worth, abilities, and value. This internal self-perception often reflects deep-seated core beliefs that influence how individuals interpret their experiences and interactions with the world around them. In contrast, the 'world' component refers to an individual's interpretation of external events, circumstances, and other people. This aspect highlights the significance of subjective perception and attribution of meaning to various stimuli, leading to cognitive biases and distorted interpretations. Finally, the 'future' component reflects an individual's expectations and predictions about what lies ahead. It encompasses thoughts related to one's anticipated outcomes, achievements, and possibilities, which may stem from past experiences or perceived limitations. The interconnectedness of these three components creates a framework through which individuals process information, construct meaning, and form cognitive patterns that can contribute to the onset and maintenance of depressive symptoms.

In comparing these components, it becomes apparent that the cognitive triad operates as an interdependent system wherein each component influences and interacts with the others. For instance, negative self-perceptions may lead to pessimistic interpretations of external events (world) and future expectations, resulting in a perpetuating cycle of negative cognition. Similarly, an individual's bleak outlook on the future can impact their self-image and how they perceive the world, further reinforcing maladaptive cognitive patterns. Understanding the comparative dynamics among these components allows for targeted interventions within cognitive therapy. By identifying how negative distortions in one component can propagate across the triad, therapists can address specific cognitive patterns and their interconnected influences. Moreover, recognizing the reciprocal relationships between these components can guide the implementation of therapeutic techniques aimed at modifying maladaptive cognitive schemas and fostering more adaptive and balanced cognitive processing. Additionally, this comparative overview underscores the importance of addressing all three components when conceptualizing and treating depressive cognitive patterns, highlighting the comprehensive nature of cognitive therapy in targeting multifaceted cognitive distortions.

5. Empirical Studies Supporting the Cognitive Triad:

Over the past few decades, numerous studies have demonstrated strong correlations between dysfunctional thought patterns regarding self, world, and future, and the onset and maintenance of depressive symptoms. Researchers have employed various methodologies, including cross-sectional surveys, longitudinal studies, experimental manipulations, and neuroimaging techniques, to investigate the complex interplay among the components of the cognitive triad and their impact on individuals' emotional well-being. The findings from these studies consistently highlight the interconnectedness of negative self-schemata, pessimistic interpretations of events, and bleak expectations for the future, providing robust support for Beck's cognitive theory of depression. One notable area of focus has been the role of early maladaptive schemas in shaping an individual's cognitive triad, with longitudinal studies demonstrating the influence of these deep-seated beliefs on the development and persistence of depressive symptoms. Furthermore, advances in neuroscientific research have shed light on the neural correlates of the cognitive triad, elucidating the underlying brain mechanisms involved in processing self-referential information, attributing meaning to environmental stimuli, and projecting future scenarios. These neuroimaging studies have bolstered the cognitive theories of depression by providing objective evidence of the neurocognitive basis of the triad's operation in the human brain.

Notably, intervention studies using cognitive restructuring techniques have yielded promising results in modifying dysfunctional cognitions related to the triad, leading to significant reductions in depressive symptomatology. These findings underscore the practical relevance of the cognitive triad model in clinical settings and emphasize the potential for targeted cognitive interventions to ameliorate depressive cognitive biases. Moreover, the collective body of empirical research has informed the refinement and elaboration of the cognitive triad model, enriching our understanding of the nuanced interactions among its components and their implications for psychological interventions.

6. Critiques and Limitations of the Cognitive Triad Model:

The Cognitive Triad model, while pioneering in its approach to understanding depressive cognition, is not without its criticisms and limitations. One notable critique pertains to the generalizability of the triad components across different cultures and socioeconomic backgrounds. Critics argue that the emphasis on self, world, and future may not accurately capture the nuances of cognitive processes in diverse populations, thereby limiting the model's applicability in a global context.

Another prominent limitation of the Cognitive Triad model is its static nature. The framework primarily focuses on the interplay between fixed components without sufficiently accounting for the dynamic nature of cognitive patterns and their evolution over time. Furthermore, some researchers have raised concerns about the oversimplification of complex cognitive phenomena, noting that the triad might overlook complex cognitive mechanisms that contribute to depressive symptomatology.

Additionally, scholars have highlighted the challenge of disentangling causation from correlation within the cognitive triad. While empirical evidence supports associations between negative cognitions and depression, establishing a causal relationship remains elusive. This raises questions about whether the cognitive triad components are primarily causal drivers of depression or if they reflect consequences of underlying mood disturbances.

Critics also point to the potential for self-fulfilling prophecies within the cognitive triad framework. By fixating on negative beliefs about the self, world, and future, individuals may inadvertently reinforce these cognitions through selective attention and interpretation of experiences, perpetuating a cycle of negativity and reinforcing depressive symptoms.

The Cognitive Triad model has been scrutinized for its comparative neglect of physiological and social factors in influencing depressive cognitions. Researchers contend that the model's exclusive focus on cognitive processes may overlook the interplay of biological, environmental, and interpersonal influences on depressive symptom development and maintenance.

Lastly, the Cognitive Triad model's therapeutic implications have faced scrutiny, with some practitioners expressing reservations about the efficacy of exclusively targeting cognitive distortions without addressing broader contextual factors contributing to depression.

In light of these critiques and limitations, it is essential to critically evaluate and refine the Cognitive Triad model, considering alternative frameworks and integrating multidimensional perspectives to enhance our understanding of depressive cognition.

7. Linking the Cognitive Triad to Depression Symptoms:

Understanding the relationship between the cognitive triad and depression symptoms is imperative in elucidating the underlying mechanisms of depressive disorders. The cognitive triad, encompassing a person's views of themselves, their world, and their future, has been found to play a fundamental role in shaping the experience and expression of depressive symptoms. As individuals perceive themselves negatively, alongside holding pessimistic views of the external world and anticipating bleak future outcomes, a complex interplay transpires, contributing to the manifestation and perpetuation of depressive symptomatology.

An individual's negative self-perception within the cognitive triad is closely linked to feelings of worthlessness, inadequacy, and self-criticism, commonly observed in individuals with depression. Furthermore, distorted beliefs about the world as inherently harsh, uncaring, or hopeless often correlate with an individual's heightened experiences of sadness, hopelessness, and despair. Likewise, pessimistic predictions regarding the future engender feelings of helplessness and lack of motivation, hallmark attributes of depressive symptomatology. Therefore, by recognizing the impact of each component of the cognitive triad on depression symptoms, clinicians and researchers can gain valuable insights into the underlying cognitive processes at play in depression.

Extensive empirical evidence has substantiated the significance of the cognitive triad in shaping the severity and persistence of depression symptoms. Studies have consistently demonstrated that individuals endorsing more negative cognitive triad beliefs tend to exhibit heightened levels of depressive symptoms, including persistent sadness, diminished interest or pleasure, changes in appetite or weight, disturbances in sleep, psychomotor agitation or retardation, fatigue or loss of energy, feelings of worthlessness or excessive guilt, diminished ability to think or concentrate, and recurrent thoughts of death or suicide. By elucidating these associations, we can enhance our understanding of the cognitive underpinnings of depression and develop targeted interventions to alleviate the burden of depressive symptoms.

Identifying the specific dimensions of the cognitive triad that contribute most prominently to distinct depression symptoms has profound implications for personalized treatment approaches. Tailoring therapeutic interventions to restructure maladaptive beliefs about the self, the world, and the future holds promise in ameliorating specific depression symptoms in individuals.

Integrating cognitive restructuring techniques within psychotherapeutic modalities can effectively challenge and modify negative cognitive triad schemas, consequently alleviating the associated depressive manifestations. Through this comprehensive exploration of the links between the cognitive triad and depression symptoms, we aim to pave the way for innovative and tailored interventions that address the cognitive underpinnings of depression.

## Negative Views on the Self - Core Beliefs and Their Influence

1. Historical Context and Development of Negative Self-Views:

Throughout history, various philosophical and psychological perspectives have contributed to our understanding of self-views and their impact on mental health. From ancient philosophical teachings that emphasized the importance of self-reflection and virtuous living to early psychoanalytic theories that delved into the unconscious mind, the evolution of thought on self-views has been extensive and multifaceted. For instance, early philosophers such as Socrates and Plato explored the concept of self-knowledge and the influence of individual perceptions on well-being, laying the groundwork for the understanding of negative self-views as a significant factor in psychological distress. Furthermore, the emergence of psychoanalysis through the works of Freud and Jung highlighted the role of childhood experiences and internal conflicts in shaping an individual's perception of self. This emphasis on early developmental influences continues to resonate in contemporary discussions on core beliefs. The subsequent development of cognitive theories, particularly Beck's cognitive theory of depression, brought to light the direct link between negative self-views and the onset and maintenance of depressive symptoms. This historical context underscores the significance of negative self-views and core beliefs in psychological discourse. The interplay between historical insights and modern research provides a comprehensive framework for understanding the development of negative self-views and their impact on individuals' mental well-being.

## 2. Core Beliefs in Clinical Practice:

Core beliefs, also referred to as schemas, are deeply ingrained cognitive structures that shape an individual's perception of themselves, others, and the world. These beliefs are often formed in early childhood and adolescence, arising from significant experiences and interactions with caregivers, peers, and societal influences. They represent fundamental assumptions about oneself and others, often operating at a subconscious level and influencing perceptions, emotions, and behavior. Given their pervasive impact, accurate identification of core beliefs is central to developing effective interventions and promoting cognitive restructuring. In clinical practice, several strategies are employed to identify these deeply embedded cognitive structures. One approach involves utilizing structured interviews and self-report measures designed to elicit core beliefs related to self-worth, personal competence, and social acceptance. Additionally, therapists may explore recurrent themes in an individual's narratives and examine patterns of automatic thoughts and emotional reactions in various situations. Collaborative exploration and validation of these beliefs within the therapeutic relationship are also foundational in this process. It is important to recognize that core beliefs can manifest in a variety of forms, such as 'I am unlovable,' 'I am incompetent,' or 'I am powerless.' These pervasive convictions often underpin specific cognitive distortions and maladaptive coping strategies. Furthermore, core beliefs may be intertwined with other cognitive constructs, such as intermediate beliefs and conditional assumptions, adding layers of complexity to their identification. The identification of core beliefs in clinical practice requires sensitivity, empathy, and patience, as individuals may experience distress and resistance when confronting deeply held negative self-appraisals. Moreover, cultural considerations and contextual factors must be taken into account to ensure a comprehensive understanding of the individual's belief system. Ultimately, by skillfully identifying and addressing core beliefs, clinicians can pave the way for profound shifts in self-perception and contribute to the alleviation of depressive symptomatology.

3. Cognitive Distortions and Their Role in Self-Perception:

Cognitive distortions, as elucidated within the framework of cognitive theory, represent biased and irrational patterns of thinking that lead individuals to perceive reality inaccurately. When applied to self-perception, these distortions play a pivotal role in shaping how individuals evaluate themselves and their abilities. At the core of cognitive distortions is the tendency to filter information through skewed mental filters, leading to subjective interpretations of events and experiences. These distortions often manifest in numerous forms, such as personalization, polarized thinking, and overgeneralization, all of which contribute to a distorted self-image.

The impact of cognitive distortions on self-perception cannot be understated. For instance, personalization occurs when individuals interpret external events as being unduly related to themselves, leading to an exaggerated sense of responsibility for outcomes. Likewise, polarized thinking, also known as black-and-white thinking, fuels self-perception by categorizing experiences as entirely positive or negative, leaving little room for nuance or complexity in self-evaluation. Overgeneralization, another common distortion, involves drawing overarching conclusions about the self based on limited evidence or isolated incidents, thereby perpetuating a skewed self-appraisal.

In the context of depression, individuals with pervasive cognitive distortions often engage in negative self-talk and harbor deeply ingrained beliefs that reinforce and perpetuate their distorted perceptions. These distortions engender a self-reinforcing cycle, wherein negative self-perceptions give rise to negative emotions, which, in turn, further confirm and solidify these maladaptive beliefs. The ramifications are far-reaching, influencing various aspects of an individual's life, including interpersonal relationships, professional endeavors, and overall well-being.

Recognizing and addressing cognitive distortions within the sphere of self-perception is an essential aspect of cognitive-behavioral interventions aimed at ameliorating depressive symptoms. Therapeutic techniques, such as cognitive restructuring, serve to challenge and reframe distorted thoughts, thereby fostering a more balanced and realistic self-view. By systematically examining and modifying cognitive distortions, individuals can gradually shift from a negative self-appraisal to a more accurate and constructive assessment of themselves, ultimately laying the groundwork for improved emotional well-being and psychological resilience.

4. Mechanisms Underlying Negative Self-Appraisal:

Negative self-appraisal, a key component of cognitive theories of depression, is driven by complex cognitive and emotional mechanisms. These mechanisms play a significant role in shaping an individual's perception of themselves and their place in the world. One fundamental mechanism underlying negative self-appraisal is the cognitive process of selective abstraction, where individuals focus on isolated negative aspects of themselves while disregarding positive or neutral experiences. This bias leads to an overemphasis on perceived failures and inadequacies, contributing to a distorted self-image. Additionally, individuals struggling with negative self-appraisal often engage in overgeneralization, extrapolating specific instances of failure to global conclusions about their worth and capabilities. This cognitive distortion amplifies feelings of worthlessness and hopelessness, further reinforcing the negative self-view. Furthermore, the mechanism of dichotomous thinking, or 'black-and-white' thinking, contributes to negative self-appraisal by fostering extreme evaluations of one's actions and characteristics as either purely positive or entirely negative, without recognizing the nuances and complexities of human experience. This rigid thinking pattern exacerbates self-criticism and undermines resilience. Emotion regulation also plays a pivotal role in negative self-appraisal, as individuals may struggle to manage distressing emotions linked to perceived shortcomings and failures. Chronic emotional dysregulation can perpetuate a self-reinforcing cycle, wherein negative self-beliefs lead to increased emotional distress, which, in turn, reinforces the negative self-views. Finally, social comparison processes, both offline and in today's digital age, often serve as triggers for negative self-appraisal. Individuals may unfavorably compare their accomplishments, appearance, or lifestyles to those of others, leading to feelings of inadequacy and inferiority. Recognizing and understanding these complex mechanisms allows clinicians and individuals alike to address negative self-appraisal effectively. By targeting these underlying cognitive and emotional processes, interventions tailored to modify these maladaptive patterns can promote more adaptive self-perceptions and contribute to alleviating depressive symptoms.

5. Empirical Evidence on Core Belief Dynamics:

Empirical evidence on core belief dynamics provides invaluable insights into the cognitive processes underlying negative self-appraisal in individuals experiencing depression. Research within the field of clinical psychology has yielded a plethora of studies elucidating the nature and influence of core beliefs on emotional functioning and psychological well-being. Studies employing various methodologies, including longitudinal assessments, experimental manipulations, and neuroimaging techniques, have contributed to our understanding of how core beliefs develop, interact with other cognitive processes, and impact affective states. Longitudinal investigations have revealed the persistence of negative core beliefs over time, highlighting their stable influence on an individual's cognitive schema. Additionally, experimental research has demonstrated the causal role of core beliefs in shaping emotional responses and behavioral tendencies. Moreover, advanced neuroimaging studies have provided neurobiological evidence of the neural correlates associated with the activation of negative core beliefs, shedding light on the underlying mechanisms at the brain level. Importantly, empirical evidence has indicated that core beliefs often operate outside of conscious awareness, exerting subtle yet pervasive effects on information processing and emotional reactivity. Through meticulous examination of these empirical findings, clinicians and researchers gain valuable insights into the interplay between core beliefs, cognition, and emotional experiences. Further exploration of core belief dynamics through rigorous empirical inquiry is essential for advancing our knowledge of depressive cognition and enhancing therapeutic interventions tailored to address negative self-views.

6. Impact of Early Experiences on Core Belief Formation:

The formation of core beliefs is inextricably linked to an individual's early experiences, particularly during childhood and adolescence. During these formative years, individuals are highly impressionable and vulnerable to the influence of their environment, which significantly shapes their cognitive frameworks and self-perceptions. As such, it is imperative to explore the profound impact of early experiences on the development and solidification of core beliefs.

Early experiences within the family unit play a pivotal role in shaping an individual's core beliefs. The dynamics of a person's interactions with caregivers, siblings, and other family members contribute to the formation of foundational cognitive schemas. Caregivers serve as primary attachment figures, and their responsiveness, support, and validation significantly influence a child's sense of self-worth and competence. Conversely, experiences of neglect, rejection, or maltreatment can engender negative core beliefs centered on unworthiness, unlovability, and helplessness. Furthermore, witnessing interpersonal conflicts or experiencing familial trauma can foster distorted perceptions of relationships and the world, perpetuating maladaptive core beliefs.

Beyond the family environment, broader societal factors and cultural influences also shape core beliefs. Socialization processes within schools, peer groups, and communities impart norms, values, and expectations that mold an individual's self-concept. Persistent exposure to discrimination, bullying, or marginalization can foster deep-seated beliefs of inadequacy, inferiority, or alienation. Adverse societal conditions, such as poverty, instability, or violence, may reinforce feelings of powerlessness and hopelessness, fueling the adoption of negative core beliefs that persist into adulthood.

Psychological theories, including attachment theory and social learning theory, offer valuable insights into the mechanisms through which early experiences influence core belief formation. Attachment theory posits that early relational experiences shape internal working models, influencing subsequent relationships and self-views. Social learning theory highlights the role of observational learning and reinforcement in acquiring and internalizing beliefs about oneself and the world. These theoretical frameworks underscore the impact of early experiences on the cognitive architecture of individuals.

Understanding the impact of early experiences on core belief formation is indispensable in clinical practice. Therapeutic interventions aimed at addressing maladaptive core beliefs must consider the nuanced interplay between past experiences and present cognitive schemas. By exploring and processing early experiences, individuals can gain insight into the origins of their core beliefs, paving the way for cognitive restructuring and the cultivation of adaptive self-perceptions. Moreover, interventions targeting children and adolescents hold promise in preventing the entrenchment of detrimental core beliefs, offering opportunities for early intervention and positive developmental trajectories.

7. Clinical Vignettes - Manifestations of Negative Self-Views:

In clinical practice, the manifestations of negative self-views are diverse and profound. One common manifestation is a pervasive sense of worthlessness and inadequacy that colors an individual's perception of themselves and their abilities. This can lead to a distorted self-image, with individuals perceiving themselves as fundamentally flawed or unlovable. Such negative self-views often contribute to persistent feelings of hopelessness and despair, undermining an individual's sense of agency and self-efficacy.

Another prominent manifestation involves recurrent self-critical thoughts and a tendency to ruminate on past failures or perceived shortcomings. These internalized criticisms can be relentless, shaping one's inner dialogue and eroding self-confidence. Individuals experiencing this may also exhibit patterns of self-sabotage, avoiding challenges or opportunities for fear of confirming their negative beliefs about themselves. Such behavior perpetuates a self-fulfilling prophecy, reinforcing and validating the negative self-views.

Negative self-views often manifest in interpersonal relationships, as individuals may struggle with forming and maintaining meaningful connections. They may perceive themselves as burdensome, unworthy of love, or incapable of establishing fulfilling relationships. Consequently, these individuals may withdraw from social interactions, leading to isolation and further reinforcing their negative self-views.

Additionally, individuals with negative self-views may engage in maladaptive coping mechanisms, such as substance abuse or self-harm, as a means of temporarily alleviating their emotional distress. This can further entrench the negative self-views and create additional barriers to seeking help and support.

Some individuals may manifest their negative self-views through perfectionistic tendencies, relentlessly pursuing unattainable standards in a quest for validation and acceptance. This perfectionism can be paralyzing, leading to avoidance of tasks and experiences where they fear failure, ultimately perpetuating the cycle of negative self-views.

Understanding these clinical vignettes illuminates the multifaceted impact of negative self-views on individuals' emotional well-being and functioning. Recognizing these manifestations is essential in guiding effective therapeutic interventions aimed at addressing and modifying these entrenched beliefs.

8. Therapeutic Strategies for Core Belief Modification:

The process of identifying and reshaping deeply ingrained negative self-views requires a well-defined framework and a range of empirical-based techniques. The collaborative empirical work of prominent researchers such as Aaron and Judith Beck, coupled with extensive clinical observations, highlights the significance of addressing core beliefs within the therapeutic milieu. Understanding that core beliefs are deeply entrenched cognitive structures vital to one's self-concept forms the foundation for effective therapeutic intervention.

Cognitive restructuring serves as a fundamental technique in amending core beliefs. This approach involves challenging the accuracy and validity of maladaptive self-perceptions through empirical inquiry, critical evaluation, and reality testing. By assisting clients in evaluating the evidence supporting their negative self-views, therapists can facilitate a gradual shift towards more balanced and adaptive self-appraisals. Furthermore, encouraging clients to engage in behavioral experiments that challenge their core beliefs fosters an experiential understanding of their malleability.

An additional nuanced strategy involves fostering self-compassion and self-acceptance. Therapists prioritize creating a safe and empathetic environment wherein clients can explore the origins of their core beliefs without fear of judgment. Encouraging self-compassion cultivates an inner dialogue characterized by kindness and understanding, thereby mitigating the intensity of negative self-views. Techniques such as mindfulness-based interventions and compassionate imagery further promote a sense of self-worth and acceptance, essential in counteracting entrenched negative self-views.

Integrating schema-focused techniques into treatment plans can also be instrumental in addressing and transforming core beliefs. Engaging in schema therapy enables clients to recognize pervasive themes underlying their core beliefs and offers specific techniques to challenge and modify these enduring schemas. By elucidating the origin and maintenance of maladaptive schemas, therapists can collaboratively work with clients to construct alter native narratives that promote adaptive beliefs and behavior.

It is imperative for therapists to convey the importance of incremental change and offer consistent reinforcement of progress. Establishing realistic expectations and acknowledging the resilience required to challenge entrenched core beliefs encourages a steady and sustainable pathway towards self-reappraisal. The reinforcement of small victories and the integration of positive reframing techniques further consolidate the process of core belief modification.

## Perception of the World

1. Cognitive Processes Influencing Worldview:

The cognitive processes influencing worldview in the context of depression are multifaceted and pivotal to understanding the mechanisms underlying perception. These processes mold an individual's interpretations, assumptions, and evaluations of the external world, thereby significantly influencing their experiences and emotional responses. In depression, cognitive processes play a profound role in shaping how individuals perceive and interact with their surroundings.

One key cognitive process that influences worldview is selective attention. Individuals experiencing depression often demonstrate a heightened tendency to selectively attend to negative stimuli in their environment, while inadvertently neglecting or discounting positive or neutral information. This selective attention bias contributes to the perpetuation of negative perceptions of the world, reinforcing beliefs about threat, rejection, and failure.

The cognitive processes of interpretation and judgment significantly impact worldview in depression. Individuals with depressive symptoms may employ a cognitive distortion known as 'catastrophizing,' wherein they systematically perceive situations or events as significantly more negative or catastrophic than they objectively are. This distorted interpretation not only amplifies negative emotions but also reinforces maladaptive beliefs about oneself, the world, and the future.

Another vital cognitive process that influences worldview is memory retrieval and integration. In the context of depression, individuals may exhibit a recall bias favoring negative memories over positive ones. This bias further consolidates negative interpretations of past experiences, contributing to a perpetual cycle of pessimism and hopelessness.

The cognitive processes of rumination and overgeneralization play a critical role in shaping worldview. Rumination involves repetitively dwelling on negative thoughts and experiences, amplifying their emotional impact and exacerbating negative worldview perceptions. Similarly, overgeneralization leads individuals to draw sweeping conclusions about themselves or the world based on isolated instances, further solidifying negative global beliefs.

In addition, cognitive processes such as cognitive dissonance and cognitive restructuring impact worldview in depression. Cognitive dissonance arises when individuals hold conflicting beliefs about themselves and their environment, leading to psychological discomfort and a skewed perception of the world. On the other hand, cognitive restructuring techniques aim to challenge and modify entrenched negative thought patterns, thereby fostering a more balanced and adaptive worldview.

2. Relationship Between World Perception and Behavior:

Cognitive psychologists assert that an individual's perception of the external world significantly influences their behavioral responses and emotional experiences. In the context of depression, distorted perceptions of the world can lead to maladaptive behaviors and contribute to the maintenance of negative affective states.

At the core of this relationship lies the concept of cognitive biases, wherein individuals with depression display a tendency to interpret external events in a negative light. These biases can manifest as selective attention, memory distortions, and biased interpretations of ambiguous stimuli, ultimately shaping one's behavioral repertoire. For instance, individuals experiencing cognitive distortions may selectively attend to information that confirms their negative worldview while disregarding or minimizing positive or neutral stimuli. This selective focus on negative cues can fuel avoidance behaviors, social withdrawal, and decreased engagement in rewarding activities, contributing to the perpetuation of depressive symptoms.

The role of core beliefs in mediating the relationship between world perception and behavior cannot be overlooked. Core beliefs, deeply ingrained assumptions about the self, others, and the world, influence the interpretation of external events and, consequently, dictate behavioral responses. In individuals with depression, negative core beliefs may lead to self-fulfilling prophecies, where their behavior aligns with their pessimistic worldview, reinforcing the original negative belief. Consequently, these behavioral patterns can create self-perpetuating cycles of negativity, further entrenching the individual in depressive symptomatology.

Additionally, socio-cognitive factors play a crucial role in shaping the relationship between world perception and behavior in depression. Interpersonal schemas, developed through past experiences and social interactions, guide individuals' expectations and interpretations of others' behaviors. In the context of depression, negative interpersonal schemas can lead to a heightened sensitivity to perceived rejection, misinterpretation of social cues, and impaired communication, resulting in maladaptive behavioral responses such as social withdrawal and avoidance.

Understanding the complex interplay between world perception and behavior is pivotal in devising effective intervention strategies for individuals with depression. By addressing distorted cognitive processes and targeting maladaptive behaviors, clinicians can work towards modifying negative world perceptions and breaking the cycle of depressive symptom maintenance. Furthermore, cultivating adaptive coping strategies and fostering realistic interpretations of the external world can facilitate positive behavioral changes, contributing to overall improvements in mood and functioning.

3. Negative Biases in External Interpretation:

The way individuals perceive the external world is greatly influenced by cognitive biases, especially in the context of depression. Negative biases in external interpretation refer to tendencies to perceive and interpret external events, circumstances, or information in a consistently negative manner. These biases can significantly impact an individual's worldview, leading to heightened vulnerability to depressive symptoms.

One of the common cognitive biases seen in depression is selective attention toward negative stimuli. Individuals with depression tend to disproportionately focus on negative aspects of their environment while overlooking positive or neutral cues. This selective attention sustains and exacerbates negative perceptions of the world, creating a cycle of pessimism and hopelessness.

Additionally, individuals experiencing depression often exhibit a tendency towards overgeneralization. This cognitive distortion involves drawing broad, sweeping conclusions about the self, others, or the world based on limited, specific instances. For example, a person may perceive a single rejection as evidence that they are universally unlikable, contributing to a distorted and negatively biased view of their external interactions.

Another prevalent negative bias in external interpretation is the tendency to engage in mental filtering, wherein individuals with depression amplify negative details while filtering out positive or neutral information from their experiences. This filtering process reinforces negative perceptions, distorting their overall perspective of the external world.

Individuals with depression commonly experience a sense of personalization, attributing external events and outcomes to internal factors such as personal inadequacy or unworthiness. This attributional style intensifies negative biases, leading to a pervasive sense of helplessness and self-blame.

Understanding these negative biases in external interpretation is crucial in the context of cognitive therapy for depression. By identifying and challenging these distortions, individuals can begin to reframe their perceptions of the world, ultimately alleviating depressive symptoms and fostering a more balanced and adaptive perspective.

Research offers promising insights into interventions aimed at addressing negative biases in external interpretation. Techniques such as cognitive restructuring, mindfulness-based approaches, and behavioral activation have shown efficacy in modifying these biases and promoting more accurate, balanced perceptions of the external world. Integrating these strategies into therapeutic interventions can play a pivotal role in reshaping individuals' cognitive frameworks, ultimately fostering resilience against depressive tendencies.

4. Core Beliefs Shaping World Perception:

Core beliefs stem from early experiences and significantly influence how individuals interpret and interact with their surroundings. In the cognitive theory of depression, core beliefs are often characterized by their rigidity and negative orientation. Such beliefs form the lens through which individuals perceive the world, leading to distortions and misinterpretations of events and experiences. Understanding the nature and impact of these core beliefs is essential in addressing depressive cognition.

Core beliefs related to world perception often revolve around themes of safety, trust, and control. Individuals with depression may hold beliefs such as 'the world is hostile and dangerous', 'I cannot trust anyone', or 'I have no control over my circumstances'. These fundamental assumptions color their understanding of external events, leading to heightened vigilance, suspicion, and a sense of helplessness. Consequently, they may exhibit avoidance behaviors, social withdrawal, or hypervigilance in response to perceived threats, further reinforcing their negative worldview.

Core beliefs can also manifest as global attributions of personal responsibility for negative events or circumstances. Depressed individuals may internalize setbacks and failures, attributing them to inherent flaws or inadequacies within themselves. This self-blame perpetuates feelings of worthlessness and contributes to a distorted perception of the world as inherently unforgiving and unsupportive.

Addressing core beliefs shaping world perception involves cognitive restructuring and challenging maladaptive thought patterns. By identifying and examining these beliefs, individuals can gain insight into the origins of their distorted perceptions and begin to reframe their outlook. Cognitive-behavioral techniques such as Socratic questioning, evidence gathering, and behavioral experiments can aid in modifying these core beliefs, fostering a more balanced and realistic perception of the world.

Therapeutic interventions that focus on building adaptive coping strategies and enhancing resilience can help individuals counteract the pervasive influence of negative core beliefs. By cultivating a sense of agency and mastery over their experiences, individuals can gradually shift their worldview towards one that is less characterized by despair and hopelessness.

5. Role of Social Constructs in Cognitive Viewpoints:

Social constructs encompass societal norms, cultural expectations, and interpersonal dynamics, all of which contribute to an individual's perception of the world. The influence of social constructs on cognitive viewpoints becomes particularly evident when examining how individuals with depression interpret and interact with their surroundings.

In many cultures, there exists an implicit expectation for individuals to adhere to certain standards of success, happiness, and fulfillment. These expectations can inadvertently reinforce negative cognitive patterns in individuals experiencing depression. For instance, societal emphasis on achievement and productivity may exacerbate feelings of inadequacy or failure among those grappling with depressive symptoms. Consequently, these individuals may internalize societal norms, leading to distorted perceptions of themselves and the world around them.

Social constructs can perpetuate stigmatization surrounding mental health, further impacting cognitive viewpoints. Fear of judgment and rejection from society may dissuade individuals from seeking help or openly discussing their struggles, perpetuating a cycle of isolation and despair. As a result, the internalization of societal attitudes towards mental illness shapes the cognitive framework through which individuals perceive their place in the world.

Interpersonal relationships also serve as influential social constructs that shape cognitive viewpoints in depression. The dynamics within familial, romantic, and platonic relationships can significantly impact an individual's self-perception and worldview. For example, unresolved conflicts or strained relationships may foster feelings of worthlessness or unlovability, reinforcing negative core beliefs and distorting perceptions about interpersonal interactions.

The broader cultural context, including representations in media and popular culture, contributes to the formulation of cognitive viewpoints. Media portrayals often perpetuate idealized standards of beauty, success, and happiness, which can serve as triggers for individuals experiencing depressive symptoms. Additionally, underrepresentation or misrepresentation of mental health issues in media may contribute to the invalidation of internal experiences, further distorting cognitive viewpoints.

Understanding the interplay between social constructs and cognitive viewpoints is paramount in addressing depression from a holistic perspective. By acknowledging and confronting the pervasive influence of societal norms, cultural expectations, and interpersonal dynamics, it becomes possible to develop targeted interventions that address the underlying cognitive distortions perpetuated by these constructs. Through fostering awareness and empathy within societal frameworks, it is feasible to create environments that support adaptive cognitive processing and mitigate the detrimental impact of social constructs on individuals' cognitive viewpoints in the context of depression.

6. Impact of Media and Culture on Perceptual Frameworks:

The impact of media and culture on perceptual frameworks is a significant area of study in understanding how individuals perceive the world, particularly in the context of depression. Media, including television, film, and social media, often portrays an idealized or skewed version of reality, which can contribute to distorted perceptions of the world. Depressive individuals may be more susceptible to internalizing these portrayals due to their negative cognitive biases.

Cultural influences also play a crucial role in shaping perceptual frameworks. Different cultures have varying norms, values, and belief systems that influence how individuals interpret and interact with the world around them. In the context of depression, cultural factors can contribute to feelings of isolation or alienation, further reinforcing negative world perceptions.

Media and cultural influences can perpetuate societal stigmas surrounding mental health, leading individuals with depression to internalize these negative messages. This can result in a deepening of negative cognitive biases and a heightened sense of hopelessness and despair.

The ubiquity of media and the interconnectedness of global culture means that individuals are exposed to a myriad of perspectives and worldviews. This exposure can either challenge or reinforce existing cognitive frameworks, depending on the individual's receptivity and resilience.

Empirical research has demonstrated the powerful influence of media and culture on perceptual frameworks in depression. Studies have shown correlations between media consumption, cultural background, and the severity of depressive symptoms. Additionally, comparative analysis between individuals from different cultural backgrounds has revealed distinct patterns in perceptual frameworks, shedding light on the complex interplay between culture and depression.

7. Depressive Versus Healthy Perspectives:

Individuals affected by depression often exhibit cognitive biases that influence their perception of the world around them. These biases can lead to a tendency to interpret events in a negative light, overestimate the likelihood of negative outcomes, and underestimate their ability to cope with challenges. In contrast, individuals with a healthy perspective typically demonstrate more balanced and realistic interpretations of events, which contribute to a greater sense of well-being and resilience.

From a cognitive standpoint, this comparison involves examining the automatic thoughts and underlying core beliefs that shape the respective perspectives. Depressive individuals may have a heightened sensitivity to negative stimuli, resulting in an increased focus on adverse events and a tendency to overlook positive aspects of their experiences. This negative bias can significantly impact their interpretation of the world and contribute to the maintenance of their depressive symptoms.

In contrast, individuals with a healthier outlook tend to display a more adaptive pattern of thinking, characterized by an ability to acknowledge both positive and negative aspects of their experiences. They are more likely to approach situations with a balanced mindset and consider a wider range of possibilities when interpreting the world around them. As a result, they are better equipped to manage adversity and maintain a positive self-image.

The comparative analysis delves into the emotional responses associated with these different perspectives. Depressive individuals often experience heightened levels of distress and hopelessness when faced with challenges, leading to a pervasive sense of defeat and helplessness. On the other hand, individuals with a healthy perspective are better able to regulate their emotions and maintain a sense of optimism and control in challenging situations.

Empirical research has supported these observations, highlighting the distinct cognitive patterns and emotional responses associated with depressive versus healthy perspectives. By examining these differences, researchers and clinicians can gain a deeper understanding of the cognitive processes underlying depression and develop targeted interventions to address maladaptive thought patterns and biases.

8. Empirical Studies Examining World Perception in Depression:

Studies have consistently demonstrated that individuals experiencing depression tend to exhibit a heightened propensity for negative interpretations of external events and stimuli, attributing unfavorable motives or outcomes to various situations. Furthermore, these studies have indicated that individuals with depression often display an attentional bias toward identifying and dwelling on adverse aspects of their environment, while overlooking or minimizing positive stimuli. Notably, experimental paradigms utilizing visual probes and reaction time tasks have provided empirical evidence supporting the presence of such attentional biases in depressed individuals. Additionally, neuroimaging studies have bolstered these findings by revealing altered neural activation patterns in brain regions associated with perception and interpretation of external stimuli among those with depression. These neural correlates further elucidate the interconnectedness between cognitive processing and world perception in depression, shedding light on the biological underpinnings of maladaptive perception. Critical investigations have also delved into the role of early experiences and environmental factors in shaping worldview and perceptual schemas among individuals vulnerable to depression. Longitudinal studies tracking the developmental trajectory of world perception have uncovered enduring cognitive patterns that predispose individuals to adopt a pessimistic outlook and endorse negative interpretations of reality. Moreover, cross-cultural research has unearthed intriguing variations in world perception across societies, uncovering the pervasive influence of cultural contexts on shaping cognitive frameworks and emotional responses. This expansive body of empirical literature underscores the multifaceted nature of world perception in depression, emphasizing the intertwined cognitive, emotional, and environmental determinants that contribute to the maintenance of maladaptive worldviews. Moving forward, continued research endeavors aimed at elucidating the nuanced mechanisms governing perception in depression hold promise for informing targeted interventions and therapeutic approaches that effectively address distorted world perception and alleviate the burden of depressive symptomatology.

## Future Expectations and Their Impact on Depressive Cognition

1 Theoretical Foundations of Future-Oriented Thoughts:

Cognitive theories posit that an individual's beliefs and expectations about the future play a pivotal role in shaping their emotional experiences and behavioral responses. These future-oriented thoughts are influenced by one's cognitive schema, which encompass deeply ingrained patterns of thought developed over time. The anticipatory nature of depressive cognition is inextricably tied to how individuals perceive and interpret events that are yet to unfold. According to cognitive theorists, these future-oriented thoughts are shaped by underlying cognitive biases and distortions, such as selective abstraction and catastrophic thinking. Moreover, the work of Beck and his colleagues has highlighted how negative future expectations contribute to the maintenance of depressive symptoms. Through the lens of cognitive theory, the engagement with future-oriented thoughts is characterized by a heightened attention to potential threats and a tendency to discount positive outcomes. Such maladaptive cognitive processes further fuel the cycle of negative affect and pessimism. Furthermore, Beck's cognitive triad elucidates the interconnectedness of negative views about the self, the world, and the future, demonstrating the overarching influence of future expectations on one's overall cognitive framework. From an evolutionary perspective, the predisposition towards vigilance for future adversities may have adaptive value, but in the context of depression, this inclination becomes magnified and distorted. Additionally, the attributional style theory posits that individuals prone to depression tend to attribute negative events to internal, stable, and global factors, resulting in pervasive negative expectations about the future. This entrenched negativity directly impacts an individual's appraisal of their own capabilities and the potential for positive change, thus contributing to the perpetuation of depressive symptoms.

2. Impact of Pessimistic Predictions on Mental Health:

Pessimistic predictions, a hallmark of depressive cognition, exert a profound impact on mental health, influencing emotional well-being, behavior, and overall functioning. When individuals consistently anticipate negative outcomes or view the future through a lens of hopelessness, it can lead to increased feelings of anxiety, stress, and despair. This relentless pessimism often becomes an impediment to pursuing goals and engaging in activities that could foster a sense of fulfillment and accomplishment. As individuals internalize these negative predictions, it contributes to a pattern of cognitive distortions that perpetuate the cycle of depression. Moreover, the chronic reinforcement of pessimistic expectations can erode one's resilience, making it more challenging to cope with adversities and setbacks. In turn, this exacerbates the experience of depressive symptoms and may hinder progress in therapeutic interventions.

The impact of pessimistic predictions extends beyond emotional well-being, seeping into various aspects of daily life. Individuals may become less willing to take risks or explore new opportunities due to the prevailing expectation of failure or dissatisfaction. This can impede personal and professional growth, leading to feelings of stagnation and entrapment. The consequences of such avoidance behaviors can create a self-perpetuating cycle, reinforcing the individual's negative beliefs about themselves and the world.

From a physiological standpoint, the chronic anticipation of negative outcomes can contribute to heightened stress levels, impacting physical health and exacerbating existing medical conditions. Long-term exposure to psychological distress arising from pessimistic predictions may also compromise immune function and increase susceptibility to illnesses, further complicating the individual's overall well-being.

3. Cognitive Distortions Related to the Future:

Cognitive distortions often lead to a skewed perspective on the potential outcomes of future events, resulting in heightened levels of anxiety and despair. Within the sphere of cognitive behavioral theory, several distinct types of cognitive distortions have been identified that are particularly relevant to future-oriented thoughts. One such distortion is 'catastrophizing,' where individuals excessively focus on the worst-case scenarios related to future events, magnifying potential negative outcomes while discounting any positive aspects or likelihood of a more favorable outcome. This cognitive distortion can significantly exacerbate feelings of hopelessness and helplessness, thus contributing to the maintenance of depressive symptoms. Another common distortion linked to future expectations is 'fortune-telling,' wherein individuals irrationally predict negative future events without concrete evidence or basis, leading to an ongoing sense of foreboding and pessimism. These cognitive distortions create a distorted lens through which individuals view their future, fostering a cycle of negative expectations and reinforcing maladaptive beliefs about one's self, world, and future. Moreover, individuals prone to cognitive distortions related to the future often engage in mental filtering, selectively focusing on perceived negative future outcomes while disregarding any contradictory positive experiences or evidence. This selective attention further reinforces the negative bias in their future expectations, consequently perpetuating the cycle of depressive cognition. Additionally, individuals may engage in overgeneralization, wherein a single negative future event is generalized to encompass all future experiences, leading to a pervasive sense of futility and inevitability regarding positive outcomes. Overcoming these cognitive distortions requires targeted interventions aimed at challenging and restructuring maladaptive thought patterns related to the future. By employing cognitive restructuring techniques, individuals can learn to identify, challenge, and replace these distortions with more balanced and realistic interpretations of future events. Furthermore, cultivating mindfulness and cognitive defusion strategies can assist individuals in developing a more adaptive relationship with their future expectations, thereby reducing the influence of cognitive distortions on their depressive cognition.

4. Empirical Evidence on Future Expectations:

Numerous studies have sought to unravel the complex interplay between individuals' anticipations of the future and the onset or perpetuation of depressive symptoms. One prominent line of inquiry has focused on the predictive power of future-oriented thoughts in influencing an individual's emotional well-being and mental health outcomes.

Empirical investigations conducted by esteemed researchers in the field of clinical psychology have consistently demonstrated a robust association between negative future expectations and heightened vulnerability to depression. Longitudinal studies tracking individuals over extended periods have disclosed that individuals harboring pervasive negative future outlooks are at greater risk of developing and maintaining depressive symptoms. These findings underscore the profound implications of future expectations as a critical determinant of psychological distress.

Experimental studies employing diverse methodologies, including cognitive priming paradigms and scenario-based assessments, have provided compelling evidence of the detrimental effects of pessimistic future predictions on cognitive processes. Such research endeavors have illuminated the pervasive nature of cognitive distortions related to the future, elucidating how distorted perceptions of what lies ahead can engender a profound sense of hopelessness and despair.

Importantly, neuroimaging studies utilizing advanced neuroscientific techniques have enriched our understanding of the neural substrates underlying future-oriented cognition in depression. Cutting-edge investigations employing functional magnetic resonance imaging (fMRI) and electroencephalography (EEG) have offered unprecedented insights into the aberrant brain activity associated with maladaptive future expectations, highlighting the interplay between cognitive processes and neural circuitry.

Meta-analytic reviews consolidating findings from a multitude of independent studies have underscored the consistency and generalizability of the link between future expectations and depressive symptomatology across diverse populations and cultural contexts. This convergence of evidence further solidifies the significance of future expectations as a salient target for therapeutic intervention, necessitating tailored strategies to ameliorate negative future outlooks and mitigate their adverse impact on mental well-being.

5. The Role of Hopelessness in Depression:

Hopelessness stands as a significant feature within the framework of depressive cognition. It represents a pervasive sense of pessimism about the future, often characterized by a belief that one's circumstances are unlikely to improve. This cognitive distortion is closely linked to the cognitive triad and plays a pivotal role in shaping the overall depressive experience. Within the context of depression, individuals may perceive their current situations as unchangeable and themselves as powerless to alter them, perpetuating a cycle of negative expectations.

Research has consistently demonstrated the strong connection between hopelessness and severe depressive symptoms. Individuals experiencing intense feelings of hopelessness often exhibit higher levels of anhedonia, fatigue, and a greater tendency towards suicidal ideation. Moreover, a sense of hopelessness can hinder motivation for engaging in activities that may alleviate depressive symptoms, exacerbating the condition. From a cognitive perspective, hopelessness heavily influences one's interpretation of events, often leading to a distorted perception of reality and reinforcing negative core beliefs.

The impact of hopelessness on individuals with depression extends beyond the emotional sphere, permeating their cognitive processes and behavioral patterns. This profound pessimism about the future fosters a sense of entrapment and may lead individuals to interpret even positive events in a negative light. The pervasiveness of this cognitive distortion can give rise to a self-fulfilling prophecy, wherein individuals operate under the assumption that nothing will improve, consequently failing to actively seek or acknowledge positive opportunities.

The presence of hopelessness complicates the therapeutic process, as individuals may struggle to engage with interventions aimed at restructuring their cognitions. Addressing hopelessness necessitates a multifaceted approach, encompassing cognitive restructuring, fostering realistic goal-setting, and cultivating a supportive environment. By challenging maladaptive thought patterns and promoting a gradual shift towards a more balanced perspective on the future, mental health professionals can begin to counter the grip of hopelessness within the context of depression.

6. The Self-Fulfilling Prophecy of Negative Expectations:

Negative expectations play a pivotal role in shaping the experience of individuals with depression, perpetuating a cycle of negativity that influences their thoughts, emotions, and behaviors. The self-fulfilling prophecy of negative expectations is a phenomenon in which an individual's beliefs about the future directly contribute to the outcomes they experience, thereby reinforcing and perpetuating their initial negative expectations. This self-perpetuating cycle can have profound implications for the cognitive and emotional well-being of individuals struggling with depression. It is crucial to recognize the powerful influence of negative expectations and their ability to shape the trajectory of an individual's experiences. Through the lens of cognitive theory, it becomes evident that negative expectations often lead to selective perception and interpretation of events, further reinforcing the individual's pessimistic outlook. This biased processing of information serves to confirm and solidify the individual's negative expectations, creating a feedback loop that contributes to the maintenance of depressive symptoms. Moreover, the self-fulfilling prophecy of negative expectations can also influence an individual's behavioral responses, leading them to act in ways that align with their pessimistic predictions. These behaviors, in turn, can elicit social and environmental reactions that validate the individual's negative expectations, reinforcing a vicious cycle of negativity. Understanding the dynamics of the self-fulfilling prophecy within the context of depression is essential for developing effective interventions and therapeutic strategies. By identifying and challenging negative expectations, individuals can begin to break free from the self-reinforcing cycle and cultivate a more adaptive and hopeful outlook. Psychosocial interventions, such as cognitive-behavioral therapy, aim to address and reframe negative expectations by examining evidence for and against these beliefs, encouraging adaptive coping strategies, and promoting alternative interpretations of events. Additionally, fostering a sense of agency and empowerment empowers individuals to actively participate in reshaping their future expectations and altering the trajectory of the self-fulfilling prophecy. By disrupting the negative feedback loop and instilling hope, individuals can gradually attenuate the impact of negative expectations on their depressive cognition, paving the way for a more positive and fulfilling outlook on life.

7. Interventions Targeting Future-Oriented Cognitions:

Cognitive-behavioral therapy (CBT) has been instrumental in targeting future-oriented cognitions among individuals with depressive symptoms. One of the key interventions employed within the framework of CBT is cognitive restructuring, which aims to identify and challenge maladaptive thought patterns related to future expectations. Through a collaborative and systematic process, individuals are guided to recognize their negative predictions about the future and evaluate the evidence supporting these predictions. This intervention empowers individuals to develop more balanced and realistic appraisals of future events, thereby reducing the influence of distorted thinking on their emotional well-being.

Another effective intervention involves the implementation of problem-solving techniques. By encouraging individuals to engage in structured problem-solving activities, therapists equip them with skills to address potential future stressors and challenges. This approach fosters a sense of control and efficacy, enabling individuals to approach future situations with greater resilience and adaptability. Additionally, mindfulness-based interventions have demonstrated promising results in cultivating present-moment awareness and reducing excessive preoccupation with negative future outcomes. By cnhancing individuals' ability to anchor themselves in the present, mindfulness practices mitigate the impact of pessimistic future expectations on their overall mood and psychological state.

A growing body of research has investigated the efficacy of imagery-based interventions in targeting future-oriented cognitions. Guided imagery techniques involve the visualization of positive future scenarios, thus counteracting the pervasive negativity inherent in depressive cognition. In conjunction with cognitive restructuring, guided imagery serves as a potent tool for reshaping individuals' perspectives on the future and promoting a more hopeful outlook. Moreover, narrative therapy approaches offer a unique avenue for reauthoring one's future narrative, enabling individuals to construct alternative and more empowering stories about their future trajectories.

Adjunctive interventions such as behavioral activation play a pivotal role in redirecting individuals' focus from negative future expectations towards engaging in meaningful and rewarding activities in the present moment. By facilitating increased participation in positive experiences, behavioral activation serves to counteract the passivity and withdrawal often associated with depressive cognition. Importantly, these interventions are tailored to individual needs and preferences, ensuring that the therapeutic approach resonates with each person's unique cognitive landscape and personal goals.

## Development and Nature of Maladaptive Beliefs

1. Origins of Maladaptive Beliefs:

Maladaptive beliefs, deeply ingrained cognitive structures that influence an individual's perception and interpretation of experiences, are often rooted in the developmental history of an individual. The formation of maladaptive beliefs can be traced back to early childhood experiences, as well as ongoing social and environmental interactions.

Early childhood experiences play a pivotal role in shaping the foundational beliefs that individuals hold about themselves, others, and the world. During this formative period, children rely heavily on caregivers and significant others for validation, support, and guidance. Positive experiences foster a sense of self-worth, security, and optimism, while negative or traumatic experiences can instill feelings of inadequacy, fear, and pessimism. These early relational dynamics and environmental influences lay the groundwork for the development of core beliefs that can later manifest as maladaptive schemas.

Cognitive distortions, such as black-and-white thinking, catastrophizing, and personalization, often become intertwined with the formation of maladaptive beliefs. These distortions skew perceptions and reinforce negative thought patterns, contributing to the entrenchment of maladaptive beliefs. As individuals manage the complexities of adolescence and young adulthood, these cognitive distortions may become more pronounced, further solidifying maladaptive beliefs and shaping their worldview.

Additionally, the role of environmental factors, including familial dynamics, societal expectations, and cultural influences, cannot be overlooked in the genesis of maladaptive beliefs. Family systems characterized by dysfunction, neglect, or abuse can engender beliefs of unworthiness, mistrust, and helplessness. Similarly, broader societal pressures related to success, beauty standards, and achievement may fuel the development of maladaptive beliefs pertaining to inadequacy, comparison, and the fear of failure.

Genetic predispositions and temperament traits contribute to an individual's vulnerability to forming maladaptive beliefs. Research suggests that certain personality traits, such as neuroticism or introversion, may heighten the propensity to internalize negative beliefs and experiences, amplifying the impact of developmental factors in the construction of maladaptive beliefs.

2. Cognitive Distortions and Their Correlation with Maladaptive Beliefs:

Cognitive distortions, as proposed by Beck, are irrational thought patterns that lead to skewed perceptions of reality, reinforcing negative schemas and beliefs. The cognitive distortions identified by Beck and his colleagues include all-or-nothing thinking, overgeneralization, mental filtering, disqualifying the positive, jumping to conclusions, magnification and minimization, emotional reasoning, should statements, labeling and mislabeling, and personalization. These distorted thought processes significantly contribute to the formation and perpetuation of maladaptive beliefs, thereby influencing one's emotional responses and behavioral patterns.

Empirical studies have corroborated the association between cognitive distortions and maladaptive beliefs, highlighting the cognitive-affective interplay underlying depressive symptomatology. Through systematic analyses of individuals with depression, researchers have observed a consistent pattern wherein distorted thinking patterns align closely with the content of maladaptive beliefs. Additionally, longitudinal research has demonstrated the enduring nature of these cognitive distortions, indicating their sustained influence on maladaptive beliefs over time.

The bidirectional relationship between cognitive distortions and maladaptive beliefs suggests that the two constructs mutually reinforce each other, leading to a self-perpetuating cycle of negative cognitions and dysfunctional belief systems. As cognitive distortions distort one's interpretations of events, experiences, and oneself, they fuel the reinforcement of maladaptive beliefs, further entrenching negative schemas and cognitive biases.

Recognizing the correlation between cognitive distortions and maladaptive beliefs is crucial for devising targeted interventions aimed at restructuring dysfunctional thought patterns and beliefs. Therapeutic modalities such as cognitive restructuring and cognitive-behavioral therapy (CBT) emphasize the identification and modification of cognitive distortions as a fundamental strategy to ameliorate maladaptive beliefs and alleviate depressive symptoms. By targeting specific cognitive distortions and their associated maladaptive beliefs, individuals can gradually reframe their thought processes, fostering adaptive beliefs and healthier cognitive frameworks.

3. Role of Environmental Factors in Shaping Maladaptive Beliefs:

The social, cultural, and familial environment in which an individual grows up significantly impacts their cognitive framework and belief systems. These environmental influences contribute to shaping one's perspectives, attitudes, and interpretations of experiences, thereby laying the foundation for the formation of maladaptive beliefs. Family dynamics, early childhood experiences, social interactions, and societal norms all contribute to the cognitive schemas that underlie maladaptive beliefs. Family environments characterized by constant criticism, neglect, or inconsistent reinforcement can foster negative core beliefs about oneself and the world. Additionally, exposure to traumatic events or chronic stressors in the environment can fuel the development of maladaptive beliefs rooted in fear, mistrust, or helplessness. Cultural and societal factors also play a pivotal role in shaping maladaptive beliefs. Societal emphasis on achievement, perfectionism, and appearance can lead individuals to develop rigid and unrealistic standards, contributing to the formation of maladaptive beliefs related to worthlessness, inadequacy, or failure. Furthermore, societal stigma and discrimination may perpetuate negative beliefs about oneself and reinforce a sense of hopelessness. Social interactions and peer relationships are significant contributors to the formation of maladaptive beliefs. Repeated instances of rejection, betrayal, or invalidation can solidify negative self-perceptions and foster mistrust in others, further entrenching maladaptive beliefs.

4. Genetic Influences on Cognitive Vulnerability:

Research in the field of psychology and genetics has demonstrated that genetic variations can contribute to cognitive vulnerabilities, which may increase the risk of developing maladaptive beliefs associated with depression. Understanding the interplay between genetics and cognition is essential for comprehending the complex nature of maladaptive beliefs.

The exploration of genetic influences on cognitive vulnerability involves investigating the heritability of cognitive traits related to belief formation and maintenance. Studies have identified specific genetic markers that are associated with cognitive processes such as attention, memory, and information processing styles, which are closely linked to the development of maladaptive beliefs. Moreover, twin studies have provided compelling evidence for the heritability of cognitive vulnerabilities, indicating that genetic factors significantly contribute to individual differences in belief systems.

Advances in molecular genetics have led to the identification of candidate genes that are implicated in cognitive functioning and emotional regulation. These genes can influence neurotransmitter systems, neuroplasticity, and stress reactivity, all of which are integral components of cognitive vulnerability. The interactions between these genetic factors and environmental experiences further shape an individual's cognitive predispositions, making them more susceptible to maladaptive belief systems in the face of adversity.

Importantly, understanding genetic influences on cognitive vulnerability does not imply determinism, but rather highlights the complex interaction between genetic predispositions and environmental influences. Individuals with certain genetic profiles may exhibit heightened sensitivity to negative stimuli or increased reactivity to stress, which can contribute to the formation and reinforcement of maladaptive beliefs. However, it is crucial to emphasize that genetic predispositions do not predestine individuals to develop maladaptive beliefs, as environmental factors and psychological processes also play pivotal roles in belief formation and resilience.

5. The Persistence of Dysfunctional Thought Patterns:

Dysfunctional thought patterns, once established, often exhibit a remarkable persistence that can significantly impact an individual's cognitive and emotional functioning. These entrenched cognitive patterns, shaped by experiences and reinforced through ongoing interpretations, continue to influence one's perception of self, the world, and the future.

One reason for the persistence of dysfunctional thought patterns is their reciprocal relationship with emotions. When individuals experience negative emotions, such as sadness or anxiety, it can reinforce the underlying negative beliefs, leading to a cyclical pattern of distorted thinking and heightened emotional distress. This perpetuation of negative thought-emotion cycles contributes to the maintenance of dysfunctional cognitive patterns over time.

Cognitive biases, including selective attention and memory recall, play a pivotal role in perpetuating dysfunctional thought patterns. Individuals with depression tend to selectively attend to information consistent with their negative beliefs while disregarding or downplaying contradictory evidence. This biased processing of information reinforces negative schemas and further entrenches maladaptive beliefs, thereby sustaining the dysfunctional cognitive patterns.

Additionally, the cognitive-evaluative processes involved in maintaining dysfunctional thought patterns often operate outside conscious awareness. Automatic thoughts, stemming from deeply ingrained beliefs, arise rapidly and seem reflexive, making it challenging for individuals to recognize and challenge their irrational nature. As a result, these automatic thoughts become deeply embedded in the individual's cognitive functioning, contributing to the endurance of dysfunctional thought patterns.

The environmental context in which individuals with maladaptive beliefs are embedded can reinforce and perpetuate such beliefs. Persistent exposure to adverse life events, chronic stressors, or unsupportive social environments may serve to validate and solidify negative beliefs, contributing to the resistance of change in cognitive patterns.

It is essential to understand that the persistence of dysfunctional thought patterns manifests not only in the cognitive domain but also in behavior. These persistent cognitive patterns influence an individual's behavioral responses, leading to withdrawal, avoidance, and other maladaptive coping strategies that perpetuate the cycle of negative thinking.

6. Interplay Between Personality Traits and Maladaptive Beliefs:

Personality traits play a significant role in shaping an individual's cognitive patterns, including the formation and maintenance of maladaptive beliefs. The interplay between personality and maladaptive beliefs is complex and multifaceted, often influencing each other in a reciprocal manner. Understanding this interplay is crucial in comprehending the etiology and persistence of maladaptive beliefs.

One important aspect of this interplay is the influence of personality traits on the interpretation of experiences and events. Individuals with certain personality tendencies, such as high levels of neuroticism or perfectionism, may be more prone to developing maladaptive beliefs due to their habitual patterns of interpreting situations in a negative light. For example, a person with high levels of neuroticism may be predisposed to constantly anticipate negative outcomes, leading to the formation of pessimistic and distorted beliefs about themselves, others, and the world.

Specific personality traits can act as vulnerability factors that predispose individuals to developing maladaptive beliefs in the face of adverse life events. For instance, individuals with an avoidant attachment style characterized by fear of rejection and low self-worth might be particularly susceptible to forming maladaptive beliefs about themselves and their relationships following instances of rejection or failure.

Conversely, maladaptive beliefs can also shape an individual's personality and behavioral tendencies. Over time, internalizing negative and distorted beliefs can contribute to the amplification of certain maladaptive personality traits. For instance, persistent beliefs of personal inadequacy can reinforce feelings of insecurity and self-doubt, thereby perpetuating behaviors associated with avoidant or anxious personality traits.

The interplay between personality traits and maladaptive beliefs extends beyond the individual level to interpersonal dynamics and social interactions. The presence of maladaptive beliefs can influence how individuals engage with others, affecting communication styles, conflict resolution strategies, and relationship satisfaction. Similarly, individuals' personalities can impact the reception and interpretation of feedback and validation from their social environment, further reinforcing or challenging existing maladaptive beliefs.

7. Influence of Social Interactions on Belief Formation:

Social interactions serve as a powerful medium through which individuals internalize feedback, opinions, and societal norms. During formative years, children rely on interactions within their family, peers, and educational institutions to construct their understanding of self and the world. Positive and validating interactions can foster adaptive beliefs, while negative or critical interactions may contribute to the internalization of maladaptive beliefs. These beliefs are often reinforced and perpetuated through ongoing social interactions, creating a cyclical pattern that sustains dysfunctional thought processes.

The influence of social comparison cannot be overstated. Individuals compare themselves to others within their social circles, leading to the adoption of comparable belief systems. This process is particularly relevant in the age of social media, where idealized representations and curated lifestyles can exacerbate feelings of inadequacy and promote the adoption of maladaptive beliefs. Furthermore, societal norms and cultural expectations significantly shape belief systems, as individuals strive to conform to perceived standards of success, beauty, and happiness propagated within their social milieu.

Social support and validation also hold considerable weight in belief formation. Supportive, empathetic interactions can serve as a buffer against the development of maladaptive beliefs, whereas lack of positive reinforcement or invalidating responses may reinforce existing negative beliefs. The quality of social relationships, including familial, peer, and romantic relationships, influences the degree to which maladaptive beliefs are sustained or challenged. For instance, individuals entrenched in toxic or abusive relationships may internalize harmful beliefs about themselves, perpetuating a cycle of negative cognition.

8. Transition of Maladaptive Beliefs Across Lifespan:

Maladaptive beliefs exhibit a remarkable capacity for persistence and transformation across the lifespan. Understanding the dynamic nature of maladaptive beliefs is crucial in elucidating their impact on mental health outcomes over time. During childhood and adolescence, maladaptive beliefs may originate in response to early experiences, such as adverse family dynamics, peer relationships, or academic challenges. As individuals transition into young adulthood, these beliefs can evolve in the face of changing social roles, educational pursuits, and career aspirations. The influence of societal norms and cultural expectations further shapes the trajectory of maladaptive beliefs during this phase of life. It is essential to recognize that transitions into adulthood entail significant cognitive, emotional, and identity-related adjustments, which can fuel the persistence or modification of maladaptive beliefs. Moreover, as individuals progress through middle and late adulthood, life events such as career changes, relationship developments, and health concerns may trigger shifts in maladaptive beliefs. Retirement, caregiving responsibilities, and aging-related changes can prompt reflections on one's self-concept and future expectations, thereby influencing the nature and perpetuation of maladaptive beliefs. Additionally, the prevalence of comorbid medical conditions and the manifestation of existential concerns in later life stages contribute to the evolution of maladaptive beliefs. Consequently, therapeutic interventions aimed at addressing maladaptive beliefs must be tailored to consider their nuanced developmental trajectories. Integrating lifespan perspectives into cognitive interventions allows for the identification of critical periods for intervention and the utilization of age-appropriate strategies. Moreover, fostering resilience and adaptive cognitive restructuring techniques can mitigate the influence of maladaptive beliefs across different life stages. Clinicians and researchers alike are encouraged to adopt a lifespan-oriented approach when conceptualizing, assessing, and treating maladaptive beliefs, thereby enriching the efficacy and relevance of cognitive-based interventions across the continuum of human development.

## Interrelationship Between Cognition and Emotion in Depression

1. Introduction to Cognitive and Emotional Constructs:

Cognitive constructs refer to the mental processes involved in acquiring knowledge and understanding, including perception, memory, reasoning, and decision-making. In the context of depression, cognitive constructs encompass a range of thought patterns, beliefs, and interpretations that influence emotional experience and behavior. These constructs are often characterized by negative biases, distorted perceptions, and dysfunctional processing of information. Emotionally, constructs pertain to the subjective experience of feelings and affective states, encompassing a broad spectrum ranging from sadness and hopelessness to anxiety and agitation. Understanding the interplay between cognitive and emotional constructs is essential in comprehending the complexities of depressive disorders.

Key components of cognitive constructs include cognitive schemas, which are organized patterns of thought and belief systems that shape perception and interpretation of stimuli. Examples include self-schema, world-schema, and future-schema, which underpin an individual's view of themselves, their environment, and their outlook on the future. On the other hand, emotional constructs entail the appraisal and expression of emotions, such as the ability to recognize and label emotions, and the regulation of emotional responses. Both cognitive and emotional constructs interact in a dynamic manner, influencing one another and contributing to the maintenance and exacerbation of depressive symptoms.

Cognitive and emotional constructs are closely linked through various cognitive appraisal processes. Cognitive appraisals involve the evaluation of situations, events, or thoughts, and the assignment of meaning and significance to them. In the context of depression, individuals may engage in cognitive distortions, such as overgeneralization, personalization, or catastrophic thinking, leading to maladaptive emotional responses. For instance, a negative interpretation of a specific event may trigger intense feelings of sadness or despair, perpetuating a cycle of negative cognition and emotion.

The role of core beliefs in shaping cognitive and emotional constructs cannot be overlooked. Core beliefs are deeply ingrained, fundamental assumptions about oneself, others, and the world, often developed early in life and reinforced through repeated experiences. These beliefs strongly influence cognitive and emotional processes, serving as perceptual filters through which individuals interpret their experiences. When core beliefs are negative or maladaptive, they can significantly impact the development and maintenance of depressive symptoms, shaping the individual's cognitive and emotional landscape.

## 2. Theoretical Foundations of Cognitive-Emotional Interactions:

The relationship between cognition and emotion forms the cornerstone of understanding the psychological processes underlying depression. At its core, this interplay is shaped by various theories and models that have been proposed to delineate how cognitive and emotional factors influence one another in the context of depressive disorders. One fundamental theoretical foundation is the cognitive theory put forth by Aaron Beck, which underscores the pivotal role of dysfunctional thought patterns and their impact on emotions. According to this theory, maladaptive cognitive schemas and negative automatic thoughts contribute to the development and maintenance of depressive symptoms. These cognitive distortions, such as catastrophizing or overgeneralization, are closely intertwined with emotional responses, perpetuating a cycle of negativity and despair. Furthermore, the transactional model of stress and coping elucidates the bidirectional nature of cognitive-emotional interactions, emphasizing that one's cognitive appraisals of a situation can significantly influence emotional experiences, and vice versa. This dynamic process shapes individuals' vulnerability to depression and their ability to effectively cope with stressors. Moreover, the affective neuroscience perspective posits that cognitive and emotional domains are interconnected at a neurobiological level, involving specific neural circuits and neurotransmitter systems. Such an understanding is instrumental in elucidating the underpinnings of mood disturbances and facilitating targeted interventions. Additionally, the interpersonal theories of depression highlight the significance of cognitive biases and emotional regulation in interpersonal functioning, shedding light on how dysfunctional cognitive patterns impact social interactions and relationships, thereby exacerbating depressive symptoms. These theoretical underpinnings collectively underscore the complex, bidirectional nature of cognitive-emotional interactions in the onset and perpetuation of depression, offering crucial insights for both theoretical advancements and clinical interventions.

### 3. Mechanisms Linking Cognition and Emotion:

The mechanisms linking cognition and emotion in the context of depression are complex and multifaceted, shedding light on the interplay between these two domains. One fundamental mechanism is the cognitive appraisal process, wherein individuals evaluate and interpret external events or internal thoughts, leading to the elicitation of emotional responses. The interpretation of an event or situation through a negative cognitive bias can trigger heightened emotional reactivity, particularly in depression. Additionally, attentional biases play a crucial role in directing cognitive resources towards negative stimuli, thereby influencing emotional experiences. This selective attention towards negative cues can exacerbate depressive symptoms, highlighting the profound impact of cognitive processes on emotional states. Furthermore, memory biases, such as the enhanced recall of negative memories compared to positive ones, contribute to the maintenance of depressive affect by perpetuating negative cognitive schemas and emotional distress. In addition to these cognitive processes, the role of core beliefs and cognitive distortions cannot be understated in understanding the mechanisms linking cognition and emotion in depression. Maladaptive core beliefs, stemming from early experiences, shape one's perception of the self, world, and future, consequently influencing emotional experiences. Cognitive distortions, such as black-and-white thinking, catastrophizing, and personalization, further exacerbate emotional disturbances and perpetuate depressive cycles. Importantly, these mechanisms interact bidirectionally, with cognitive processes influencing emotional experiences and vice versa. For instance, intense emotional states can lead to further reinforcement of negative cognitive patterns, creating a self-perpetuating cycle of cognitive-emotional interactions. Moreover, the individual differences in cognitive styles and emotion regulation strategies modulate the impact of these mechanisms, underscoring the importance of considering personalized approaches in addressing cognitive-emotional interactions in depression.

4. Cognitive Distortions and Emotional Responses:

Cognitive distortions, as conceptualized within the framework of cognitive theory, refer to the biased thought patterns that individuals with depression often exhibit. These distortions can lead to negative interpretations of events, interactions, and the self, contributing to a heightened emotional response. In this complex interplay between cognition and emotion, specific cognitive distortions have been identified as influential factors in shaping emotional experiences among individuals with depression. Common cognitive distortions include but are not limited to: filtering (focusing only on negative aspects while disregarding positive elements), polarized thinking (viewing situations in extremes of good or bad with no middle ground), overgeneralization (making broad negative conclusions based on limited evidence), and personalization (attributing excessive responsibility for external events). Each distortion type can profoundly impact emotional responses by perpetuating negative affect and reinforcing maladaptive coping strategies. The manifestation of these distortions often leads to heightened emotional reactivity, including feelings of anxiety, sadness, anger, or hopelessness. These emotional responses, in turn, can further reinforce the negative cognitive patterns, creating a cyclical relationship between distorted cognition and escalated emotionality. Recognizing and understanding these cognitive distortions and their direct influence on emotional responses is crucial for effective intervention and treatment of depressive symptoms. Cognitive-behavioral therapies aim to address and challenge these distortions through cognitive restructuring techniques coupled with emotion-focused interventions.

5. Empirical Studies on Cognitive-Emotional Correlates:

Empirical studies have played a crucial role in advancing our understanding of the complex interplay between cognitive processes and emotional states in individuals with depression. These studies have utilized diverse methodologies, including self-report measures, behavioral experiments, neuroimaging techniques, and physiological assessments, to investigate the relationships between cognition and emotion. One key area of investigation has been the identification and measurement of specific cognitive biases and their associations with emotional experiences in depressed individuals. Research has consistently demonstrated that individuals with depression exhibit heightened attentional biases towards negative stimuli, as well as greater memory recall for negative information, compared to non-depressed individuals. Furthermore, studies have revealed a link between maladaptive cognitive patterns, such as rumination and catastrophizing, and the intensity and duration of negative emotional states in depression. The findings from these studies not only confirm the co-occurrence of cognitive distortions and heightened emotional reactivity in depression but also highlight the bidirectional nature of this relationship. Moreover, empirical research has sought to elucidate the impact of cognitive-behavioral interventions on modifying cognitive-emotional correlates in individuals with depression. Through controlled trials and longitudinal studies, researchers have provided evidence for the effectiveness of cognitive restructuring techniques in ameliorating cognitive distortions and reducing emotional distress in individuals with depression. Importantly, neurobiological investigations have also contributed to the understanding of cognitive-emotional correlates in depression by identifying neural circuits and neurotransmitter systems that underlie the interactions between cognition and emotion. Neuroimaging studies have revealed aberrant patterns of brain activation and connectivity associated with cognitive biases and emotional dysregulation, shedding light on the neural mechanisms underlying cognitive-emotional impairments in depression. Taken together, empirical studies have not only confirmed the connections between cognition and emotion in depression but have also paved the way for the development of targeted interventions aimed at addressing cognitive-emotional processes to alleviate depressive symptoms.

6. Neurobiological Perspectives on Cognitive-Emotional Interrelations:

The neurobiological underpinnings of cognitive-emotional interrelations in depression have garnered significant attention in contemporary research. Neuroimaging studies have revealed complex networks and brain regions involved in the processing of cognitive and emotional information. The role of the prefrontal cortex, particularly the dorsolateral prefrontal cortex and ventromedial prefrontal cortex, has been emphasized in regulating cognitive control and emotional responses. Dysfunction within these regions has been linked to alterations in cognitive appraisal and emotional reactivity in individuals with depression.

Studies employing functional magnetic resonance imaging and positron emission tomography have identified aberrant activity in the amygdala, hippocampus, and anterior cingulate cortex, highlighting their involvement in the manifestation of cognitive biases and heightened emotional processing seen in depression. The dysregulation of serotonin and dopamine neurotransmitter systems, as well as the hypothalamic-pituitary-adrenal axis, also plays a pivotal role in shaping cognitive-emotional interactions in depression.

Recent advancements in the field of genetics have shed light on the genetic basis of cognitive and emotional functioning, offering insights into the heritability of cognitive vulnerabilities and emotional dysregulation in depressive disorders. Research indicates that specific genetic polymorphisms related to serotonin transporters and receptors may influence an individual's susceptibility to developing maladaptive cognitive schemas and experiencing intense negative emotions.

Complementary to neurobiological investigations, electroencephalography studies have provided valuable data on neural oscillations and event-related potentials associated with cognitive processing and emotional reactivity in depression. These findings offer a comprehensive perspective on the real-time dynamics of cognitive-emotional interplay, enhancing our understanding of the temporal aspects of information processing and affective modulation.

7. Depressive Symptoms and Thought Patterns:

Depression manifests through a complex interplay of cognitive, emotional, and physiological symptoms. Clinical observations provide valuable insights into the specific thought patterns associated with depressive disorders. Key among these observations are the pervasive negative biases in information processing. Individuals with depression tend to exhibit a persistent tendency to interpret ambiguous situations in a pessimistic and self-deprecating manner. This cognitive distortion often leads to a heightened sensitivity to perceived threats and a decreased ability to derive pleasure from positive experiences. Moreover, rumination, characterized by repetitive and intrusive negative thoughts, is a common cognitive pattern observed in individuals experiencing depression. These recurring thought patterns exacerbate feelings of hopelessness and worthlessness, contributing to the maintenance of depressive symptoms. Furthermore, it is crucial to note that cognitive impairments, such as difficulties in concentration and memory, are prevalent in individuals with depression, impacting their daily functioning and overall well-being.

In clinical practice, the identification and examination of these thought patterns form the cornerstone of cognitive therapy for depression. By targeting and challenging maladaptive cognitive processes, skilled clinicians can help individuals reframe their interpretations of life events, thereby alleviating negative affect states and reducing the severity of depressive symptoms. Additionally, a comprehensive understanding of depressive thought patterns informs the selection and tailoring of therapeutic interventions. Cognitive-behavioral interventions, including cognitive restructuring and behavioral activation, are designed to directly address and modify distorted thought patterns, promoting adaptive coping and emotional regulation. Furthermore, mindfulness-based approaches have shown promise in breaking the cycle of rumination and enhancing present-moment awareness, offering an alternative pathway to disrupting depressive thought patterns.

Given the heterogeneity of depressive symptoms and thought patterns across individuals, personalized assessment and intervention strategies are essential in clinical settings. Clinicians must strive to gain a nuanced understanding of each individual's unique cognitive-emotional profile to effectively tailor treatment plans. By integrating clinical observations with empirical research findings, professionals can optimize the delivery of interventions aimed at ameliorating cognitive distortions and alleviating the burden of depressive symptoms.

8. Therapeutic Implications of Cognition-Emotion Dynamics:

Therapeutic interventions for depression often focus on targeting the interplay between cognition and emotion, as this dynamic relationship plays a pivotal role in shaping an individual's experience of depressive symptoms. Cognitive-behavioral therapy, a widely endorsed intervention for depression, underscores the significance of modifying maladaptive thought patterns to alleviate emotional distress. By identifying and challenging cognitive distortions, individuals can restructure their thinking processes, leading to more adaptive emotional responses. Therapists work collaboratively with clients to pinpoint detrimental automatic thoughts and beliefs, fostering cognitive restructuring through techniques such as cognitive reappraisal and cognitive restructuring exercises.

It is imperative to address underlying emotional schemas, which are pervasive networks of affect-laden beliefs and memories that influence an individual's perception and processing of emotional information. Integrating emotional schema-focused approaches within therapy can offer profound insights into the origins of dysfunctional emotional responses, enabling individuals to reframe deeply ingrained emotional patterns.

Mindfulness-based interventions have gained prominence in the treatment landscape, emphasizing the cultivation of non-judgmental awareness of one's thoughts and emotions. By enhancing mindfulness skills, individuals are empowered to observe cognitive and emotional processes without becoming enmeshed in them, thereby fostering greater psychological flexibility and emotional regulation.

The incorporation of emotion-focused techniques complements cognitive restructuring efforts by addressing the experiential dimension of emotional distress. Validating and processing intense emotions within the therapeutic context can engender a sense of emotional acceptance, ultimately contributing to a reduction in distress and an enhancement of overall emotional well-being.

In addition to traditional face-to-face therapy, digital mental health platforms and mobile applications have emerged as accessible mediums for delivering cognitive-behavioral interventions. These resources offer interactive tools for monitoring moods, tracking automatic thoughts, and practicing cognitive restructuring exercises, thereby extending the reach of therapeutic strategies beyond the confines of traditional clinical settings.

It is essential to recognize that the interrelationship between cognition and emotion is complex and nuanced; hence, therapeutic approaches must be tailored to address the unique cognitive-emotional profiles of individuals. By seamlessly integrating interventions that target cognitive restructuring, emotional schemas, mindfulness, and digital platforms, therapists can effectively manage the complex terrain of cognition-emotion interactions, fostering holistic recovery and emotional well-being for individuals experiencing depression.

# COGNITIVE DISTORTIONS - IDENTIFICATION AND IMPLICATIONS

## Categorization

1. Classification Frameworks and Criteria:

Cognitive distortions represent a central focus within the field of cognitive-behavioral therapy, necessitating a comprehensive understanding of their classification frameworks and criteria. The systematic organization of cognitive distortions is vital for clinicians and researchers to discern distinct patterns of maladaptive thinking prevalent in various psychological conditions, including depression, anxiety, and other mood disorders. At the core of any classification framework lie the delineation of discrete, identifiable categories and the establishment of inclusion criteria within each category. The process entails careful consideration of the defining features that distinguish one type of cognitive distortion from another, thus allowing for clear differentiation and unambiguous categorization. Furthermore, the development of these frameworks involves collaboration among experts in psychology, psychiatry, and cognitive science, ensuring that the classification criteria are anchored in empirical evidence and clinical insight. The refinement of classification criteria is an iterative process, driven by ongoing research endeavors and clinical observations. As such, the criteria for categorizing cognitive distortions are subject to periodic updates as new knowledge emerges and diagnostic techniques evolve. A critical aspect of the classification process is the recognition of variations and overlaps in cognitive distortion patterns, prompting the formulation of inclusive yet distinct criteria to capture the full spectrum of distorted thinking. Considerations of cultural, contextual, and individual differences also play a pivotal role in shaping the classification criteria, thereby acknowledging the diversity of cognitive processes across populations and within individuals. The successful construction of robust classification frameworks demands a balance between specificity and flexibility, allowing for granular distinctions while accommodating the multifaceted nature of cognitive distortions. Through this balanced approach, the classification criteria strive to capture the complexity of human cognition without oversimplification or ambiguity.

2. Common Categories of Distorted Thinking Patterns:

In examining the landscape of cognitive distortions, it becomes evident that certain patterns frequently manifest across individuals experiencing distorted thinking. These common categories provide valuable insights into the cognitive processes underlying dysfunctional beliefs and perceptions. One prevalent category is 'catastrophizing,' wherein individuals tend to magnify the significance of negative events and anticipate the worst possible outcomes. This propensity towards catastrophic thinking often leads to heightened anxiety and irrational responses to stressful situations. Another prominent category is 'black-and-white thinking,' characterized by the inclination to perceive situations in absolute, polarized terms without considering nuanced or intermediate possibilities. This cognitive distortion often results in rigid, inflexible thinking patterns and contributes to the exacerbation of emotional distress. Moreover, the category of 'personalization' involves the tendency to attribute external events to oneself disproportionately, leading to self-blame and unwarranted guilt. By recognizing these common categories of distorted thinking patterns, mental health professionals can effectively identify and address these maladaptive cognitive processes in clinical practice. Understanding the nature of these categories lays the foundation for targeted interventions and therapeutic approaches aimed at correcting cognitive distortions and promoting adaptive thinking strategies. As we delve deeper into these categories, it is crucial to consider the interplay between cognitive distortions and emotional regulation, behavior, and overall mental well-being. Each category holds implications for therapeutic interventions and guides the development of tailored treatment plans. Therefore, a comprehensive grasp of the common categories of distorted thinking patterns is essential for fostering positive psychological change and enhancing individuals' capacity for rational, balanced cognition.

3. Illustrative Examples of Each Cognitive Distortion:

In order to grasp the significance and nuanced nature of cognitive distortions, it is imperative to delve into a comprehensive exploration of illustrative examples for each distinct type. Starting with 'All-or-Nothing Thinking,' individuals who manifest this distortion tend to perceive situations in absolute, black-and-white terms, disregarding any middle ground. An example could be a person who believes that if they don't achieve perfection in a task, then their efforts are entirely worthless, leading to feelings of extreme frustration and self-criticism. Moving on to 'Overgeneralization,' consider someone who encounters a single unpleasant event and proceeds to apply it as evidence of pervasive patterns of defeat or failure in their life. This can result in a diminished sense of self-worth and reluctance to try new endeavors. 'Mental Filtering' involves the inclination to exclusively focus on negative details while filtering out any positive aspects of a situation. For instance, an individual might receive numerous compliments on their work performance but fixate only on a single critical remark, thereby undermining their confidence and satisfaction. 'Disqualifying the Positive' represents a cognitive distortion where individuals disregard or downplay positive experiences or accomplishments, attributing them to luck or external factors rather than embracing their own capabilities and efforts. This tendency can foster feelings of unworthiness and inhibit personal growth. 'Jumping to Conclusions' encompasses two subtypes, namely mind-reading and fortune-telling. Mind-reading entails presuming to know what others are thinking or feeling without concrete evidence, leading to unnecessary anxiety and strained interpersonal relations. Conversely, fortune-telling involves anticipating negative outcomes without substantiated basis, resulting in heightened stress and avoidance behaviors. The distortion of 'Magnification and Minimization' involves the amplification of one's perceived errors or flaws while minimizing personal strengths and positive attributes. This can fuel deep-seated insecurities and hinder one's ability to acknowledge achievements. Catastrophizing entails the tendency to magnify the potential adverse outcomes of events or circumstances, often leading to overwhelming anxiety and paralyzing fear. Lastly, 'Emotional Reasoning' influences individuals to equate their emotions with reality, believing that if they feel a certain way, then it must inherently reflect the truth of a situation – even in the absence of concrete evidence. Such cognitive distortions can profoundly impact an individual's emotional well-being and overall quality of life.

4. Empirical Evidence Supporting Classification:

Numerous studies have contributed to the empirical foundation of classifying cognitive distortions. Through systematic observation, researchers have documented consistent patterns in individuals exhibiting various cognitive distortions across diverse clinical and non-clinical populations. This research has facilitated the identification of distinct clusters of distorted thinking, demonstrating the robustness and generalizability of the classification framework.

Empirical investigations employing psychometric measures have consistently corroborated the presence of cognitive distortions as discrete and quantifiable constructs. Valid and reliable instruments, such as the Dysfunctional Attitude Scale (DAS) and the Automatic Thoughts Questionnaire (ATQ), have exhibited strong internal consistency and convergent validity, affirming the discriminant nature of different cognitive distortion categories.

Neuroimaging and neuropsychological studies have elucidated the neural correlates and cognitive processes associated with specific cognitive distortions. By employing advanced imaging techniques such as functional magnetic resonance imaging and electroencephalography, researchers have provided compelling evidence linking particular cognitive distortions with aberrant activation patterns in brain regions implicated in emotion regulation and decision-making. Additionally, cognitive experimental paradigms have revealed cognitive biases and information processing irregularities characteristic of distinct cognitive distortion categories.

The comprehensive integration of these diverse lines of empirical inquiry has not only enhanced the conceptual clarity of cognitive distortion classification but has also facilitated the development of targeted interventions. By identifying the unique cognitive profiles associated with different distortions, clinicians can tailor their therapeutic approaches, thereby optimizing treatment efficacy and promoting more favorable clinical outcomes.

5. Comparison with Other Psychological Models:

When examining cognitive distortions within the context of other psychological models, it becomes apparent that various theoretical frameworks offer unique insights into the nature of human thought processes and correlating behavioral patterns. For instance, the cognitive approach emphasizes how thoughts and perceptions influence emotions and behaviors, serving as a fundamental principle in understanding cognitive distortions. In contrast, behavioral models concentrate on observable actions and their reinforcement, often overlooking the cognitive processes that underpin such behaviors. By comparing these distinct paradigms, we can uncover the interconnectedness between cognitive distortions and behavioral manifestations, shedding light on the complex interplay between cognitive and behavioral theories. Furthermore, integrating cognitive distortions within the broader framework of personality theories aids in comprehending how individual differences in cognition and perception contribute to the development and maintenance of distorted thinking patterns. The psychodynamic perspective accentuates unconscious conflicts and early life experiences as influencing present mental processes, complementing the cognitive model's focus on conscious thought patterns and cognitive biases. This intersection presents an opportunity to explore the potential interdependence between cognitive distortions and deeper, underlying psychological dynamics, leading to a more comprehensive understanding of distorted thinking across different theoretical orientations. Additionally, incorporating perspectives from social and cultural psychology expands the examination of cognitive distortions to encompass societal norms, societal pressures, and interpersonal influences on cognitive processes and distorted thinking. Recognizing the diverse impact of cultural and social factors helps in contextualizing the manifestation of cognitive distortions within various cultural contexts, emphasizing the need for culturally sensitive assessment and intervention approaches in addressing cognitive distortions.

6. Clinical Observations and Expert Insights:

Clinical psychologists and mental health professionals have long been documenting the manifestation of cognitive distortions in their patients. Through meticulous case studies and longitudinal assessments, these practitioners have unraveled critical patterns and triggers associated with distorted thinking. Their astute observations shed light on the nuanced ways in which cognitive distortions interplay with various mental health conditions, substantiating the nature of this phenomenon. Furthermore, the collaborative efforts of experts from diverse psychological backgrounds have furnished valuable insights into the complex intersectionality of cognitive distortions with other psychological models. By juxtaposing cognitive theories with behavioral and psychodynamic perspectives, professionals have discerned commonalities and disparities, enriching our comprehension of cognitive distortions within a broader psychological framework. These interdisciplinary dialogues have fostered a more holistic grasp of the multifaceted nature of distorted thinking, facilitating nuanced interventions and treatment modalities. Moreover, expert insights gleaned from research endeavors and clinical experience elucidate the challenges inherent in categorizing cognitive distortions and accommodating individual variances. The recognition of diverse cognitive profiles and idiosyncratic thought patterns underscores the need for personalized therapeutic approaches that account for the unique cognitive landscapes of each individual. Additionally, expert inputs underscore the dynamic nature of cognitive distortions, emphasizing the role of context, culture, and environmental factors in shaping distorted thinking patterns. This heightened awareness prompts a reevaluation of traditional classification frameworks, advocating for a more flexible and inclusive approach that accommodates the fluidity of cognitive processes. As we delve deeper into the domain of cognitive distortions, the amalgamation of clinical observations and expert insights catalyzes a paradigm shift, propelling us towards an integrated understanding that empowers comprehensive and tailored interventions to mitigate the impact of distorted thinking on individuals' well-being.

7. Challenges in Categorization and Individual Variances:

Despite efforts to develop comprehensive frameworks, it is critical to acknowledge the inherent individual variances that manifest in the context of distorted thinking patterns. One of the primary challenges lies in the diverse and multifaceted nature of human cognition, where individuals may exhibit unique cognitive biases and distortions based on their personal experiences, cultural backgrounds, and developmental trajectories.

The dynamic interplay between cognitive distortions and emotional states complicates the categorization process. It is essential to recognize that an individual's cognitive biases can be influenced by their current emotional state, making it challenging to delineate distinct categories when facing overlapping and interacting patterns of distorted thinking. Moreover, the level of awareness and insight into one's cognitive distortions varies widely among individuals, posing a significant obstacle in accurately classifying and categorizing these phenomena.

Another prominent challenge involves the co-occurrence of multiple cognitive distortions within an individual. In clinical settings, it is not uncommon for individuals to present with a combination of distorted thinking patterns, blurring the boundaries between categories and necessitating a nuanced understanding of how these distortions coalesce within a person's cognitive schema.

Additionally, the fluidity and adaptability of cognitive distortions over time further complicate their categorization, as individuals may exhibit different patterns based on situational, environmental, or developmental factors.

Cultural and contextual influences also play a pivotal role in shaping cognitive distortions, adding another layer of complexity to their categorization. Cultural variations in thinking styles and belief systems can lead to diverse manifestations of cognitive distortions across different populations, underscoring the need for sensitivity to sociocultural factors when categorizing and addressing distorted thinking patterns.

In light of these challenges, it is imperative for researchers and practitioners to approach the categorization of cognitive distortions with a keen awareness of individual variances and the dynamic nature of these phenomena. Embracing a flexible and inclusive framework that accommodates the variability and complexity of cognitive distortions is paramount in advancing our understanding and therapeutic interventions for these pervasive cognitive phenomena.

**Mechanisms Behind Distorted Thinking**

1. Neuroscientific Perspectives on Thought Distortions:

Recent advancements in neuroscience have provided valuable insights into the underlying mechanisms of thought distortions. Neuroimaging studies have highlighted the involvement of various brain regions, such as the prefrontal cortex, amygdala, and hippocampus, in cognitive distortions. These findings emphasize the interplay between cognitive and emotional processing in shaping our thought patterns.

Neurobiological research has elucidated the impact of neurotransmitters, such as serotonin and dopamine, on cognitive function and its potential relevance to distorted thinking. The delicate balance of these neurotransmitters is crucial for maintaining adaptive cognition and emotional regulation. Dysregulation in their levels may contribute to the emergence of distorted thoughts and perceptions.

Studies employing electroencephalography and magnetoencephalography have revealed distinct neural signatures associated with different types of cognitive distortions. For instance, maladaptive schemas characteristic of certain cognitive distortions are found to correlate with specific aberrant neural oscillations and connectivity patterns. Understanding these neural correlates is pivotal for developing targeted interventions to address thought distortions at the neurobiological level.

Additionally, neuroplasticity, the brain's remarkable ability to reorganize and form new connections in response to experience, offers promising avenues for addressing thought distortions. Interventions targeting neuroplastic changes can potentially reshape dysfunctional cognitive processing and alleviate the persistence of distorted thinking patterns.

2. The Role of Automatic Thoughts:

Automatic thoughts play a fundamental role in cognitive distortions, serving as the rapid, subconscious interpretations and evaluations of our experiences. These thoughts are often deeply ingrained and occur almost instinctively in response to triggers, influencing our emotions, behavior, and perception of reality. In the sphere of cognitive theory, these automatic thoughts are pivotal in understanding how individuals process information and can often lead to distorted thinking patterns.

Often stemming from past experiences, automatic thoughts can be both positive and negative, with the latter being particularly significant in the context of cognitive distortions. They frequently arise in the form of cognitive biases, which can manifest as overgeneralizations, catastrophic thinking, or personalization. These automatic thoughts can significantly impact an individual's emotional well-being and overall mental health.

Automatic thoughts are closely intertwined with core beliefs, reinforcing preexisting schemas about oneself, others, and the world. For individuals struggling with cognitive distortions, automatic thoughts can maintain and perpetuate negative self-perceptions and pessimistic interpretations of events, further exacerbating their distress.

Understanding the role of automatic thoughts is critical for effectively addressing cognitive distortions. Cognitive-behavioral interventions often focus on identifying and challenging these automatic thoughts, aiding individuals in developing healthier thinking patterns. By recognizing and altering automatic thoughts, individuals can reduce the impact of cognitive distortions, leading to improved emotional regulation and resilience.

3. Cognitive Biases and Their Formation:

Cognitive biases represent an intrinsic aspect of human cognition, influencing the way individuals perceive, interpret, and respond to information from their environment. These biases, which are systematic patterns of deviation from norm or rationality in judgment, often arise from various sources, including past experiences, cultural influences, and societal norms. The formation of cognitive biases is a complex interplay between psychological, social, and environmental factors. At the core of their development lie the processes of neural adaptation, reinforcement, and attentional focus.

One fundamental contributor to the formation of cognitive biases is the brain's remarkable adaptability in processing and storing information, leading to the development of mental shortcuts and heuristics. These shortcuts, while efficient in handling vast amounts of data, render individuals susceptible to systematic errors in judgment. Moreover, sociocultural context significantly shapes the formation of biases, as individuals internalize societal norms, values, and expectations, which subsequently influence their cognitive processing. Consequently, biases rooted in cultural schemas and stereotypes can manifest across diverse populations, perpetuating shared misconceptions and faulty reasoning.

The emotional component of cognitive biases is pivotal in their formation. Emotional experiences, particularly those associated with threat, reward, or loss, can imprint salient memories and preferences, rendering certain stimuli and information more memorable and influential in decision-making. As a result, individuals unconsciously exhibit preferences for information that aligns with their emotional responses, perpetuating a cycle of biased perception and interpretation.

The pervasive nature of cognitive biases underscores their profound impact on daily decision-making, problem solving, and interpersonal interactions. They not only shape individual perceptions but also contribute to larger societal phenomena, such as groupthink and misinformation propagation. Understanding the formation of cognitive biases provides a crucial foundation for identifying and effectively addressing their implications across various domains, including clinical practice, organizational management, and public policy.

4. Interaction Between Emotion and Cognition:

The interaction between emotion and cognition is a crucial aspect in understanding the mechanisms behind distorted thinking. As we know, emotions play a significant role in shaping our thought processes, influencing our perceptions, decision-making, and behavior. When individuals experience heightened emotional states, such as anxiety, fear, or sadness, their cognitive processing often becomes influenced, leading to the emergence of cognitive distortions. Conversely, distorted cognitions can also evoke strong emotional responses, creating a complex interplay between the two psychological domains.

Emotional responses can impact cognitive functioning in various ways. For example, when a person experiences intense emotions, their attention may become selectively focused on information that is congruent with their emotional state while neglecting contradictory evidence. This selective attention can exacerbate cognitive biases and reinforce distorted thinking patterns. Moreover, heightened emotions can impair rational reasoning, leading individuals to rely more on heuristics and quick judgments rather than engaging in deliberate, analytical thinking.

The relationship between emotion and cognition extends to memory processes, where emotional arousal has been shown to enhance the encoding and retrieval of information associated with the emotional stimuli. As a result, individuals may vividly remember events or experiences that have elicited strong emotions, leading to potential distortions in recalling details or interpreting past scenarios.

It is important to note that not all emotional influences on cognition lead to negative outcomes. Positive emotions, for instance, can broaden an individual's problem-solving abilities, creativity, and flexible thinking, which can counteract the rigidity often observed in distorted cognitive processing. Understanding this complex interplay between positive emotions and cognition provides valuable insights into developing interventions that harness the adaptive aspects of emotional influence while mitigating the adverse effects of negative emotions on cognitive functioning.

5. Environmental Triggers and Perception Alteration:

Environmental triggers play a crucial role in shaping our perceptions and thought patterns. The stimuli present in our surroundings can significantly impact the way we interpret and process information, leading to alterations in our cognition. Numerous studies have emphasized the profound effect of environmental factors on cognitive processes, shedding light on the relationship between our surroundings and our thought patterns.

One of the key aspects of environmental triggers is their ability to elicit emotional responses, which, in turn, influence our cognitive appraisal. For instance, an individual exposed to a stressful or threatening environment may experience heightened anxiety or fear, thereby distorting their perceptions of reality. This alteration in perception can lead to cognitive biases and distorted thinking, ultimately impacting decision-making and behavior.

Environmental triggers can also shape our attentional focus and cognitive processing. External stimuli such as noise, temperature, and visual cues can modulate our attention and concentration levels, influencing the way we perceive and interpret information. Additionally, the presence of specific environmental cues linked to past experiences or traumatic events can trigger maladaptive thought patterns and cognitive distortions.

It is important to note that the influence of environmental triggers on perception alteration extends beyond immediate sensory input. Cultural, social, and contextual factors within the environment also contribute to the construction of cognitive schemas and belief systems. These ingrained frameworks can influence how individuals perceive themselves, others, and the world around them, consequently impacting their thought patterns and cognitive processing.

In light of these considerations, it becomes evident that understanding the impact of environmental triggers on perception alteration is essential in addressing cognitive distortions and promoting mental well-being. By recognizing the interplay between environmental stimuli and cognitive processes, individuals and clinicians can develop targeted interventions and environmental modifications to mitigate the adverse effects of distorted thinking.

6. Structural Models of Thought Process Disruption:

The structural models of thought process disruption provide a framework for understanding the mechanisms underlying cognitive distortions. These models aim to elucidate how certain cognitive processes deviate from their typical functionality, leading to maladaptive thought patterns and beliefs. One prominent model is the information processing model, which suggests that individuals with cognitive distortions exhibit altered processing of incoming information. This manifests in selective attention to negative stimuli, exaggeration of potential threats, and neglect of positive or neutral cues. Additionally, the parallel distributed processing model posits that cognitive distortions stem from interconnected neural networks, where maladaptive patterns of activation and inhibition contribute to distorted processing of information. Furthermore, the self-regulatory executive function model highlights deficits in cognitive control mechanisms, such as inhibitory control and cognitive flexibility, leading to perseveration on negative thoughts and limited consideration of alternative perspectives. Another crucial aspect of structural models involves the interaction between cognitive and emotional systems. The affective priming model emphasizes how heightened emotional responses can influence cognitive processing, thereby amplifying the salience of negative information and reinforcing distorted thought patterns. Moreover, the emotional cascade model underscores the cascading effect of intense emotions on cognitive functioning, resulting in cognitive rigidity and increasing susceptibility to cognitive distortions. These structural models collectively shed light on the multi-dimensional nature of thought process disruption, encompassing information processing, neural network dynamics, executive functions, and emotional influences.

7. Validation and Devaluation Mechanisms:

Validation and devaluation mechanisms are critical components in understanding the intricacies of cognitive distortions. The validation process involves a consistent reinforcement of negative beliefs and thoughts, leading to an individual's perception that these thoughts hold true significance. This mechanism contributes to the perpetuation of distorted thinking patterns and sustains the overarching cognitive biases prevalent in individuals experiencing depressive symptoms.

Conversely, devaluation mechanisms involve the dismissal or undermining of positive or constructive thoughts and experiences. Individuals exhibiting devaluation mechanisms often discount their achievements, positive feedback from others, or moments of joy, attributing disproportionate significance to negative events or self-critical thoughts. These mechanisms contribute to the maintenance of depressive symptomatology and further entrench the individual in a cycle of negative cognitions.

The intertwining of validation and devaluation mechanisms can create a reinforcing loop that amplifies the impact of cognitive distortions on an individual's emotional well-being. Such mechanisms are often deeply ingrained and may operate at a subconscious level, making them particularly challenging to address through traditional cognitive therapies without a tailored focus on these specific components.

Research in cognitive psychology has shed light on the prevalence of validation and devaluation mechanisms in individuals with depressive symptoms. Understanding these mechanisms is crucial to devising targeted intervention strategies that aim to disrupt and reframe these thought patterns. Cognitive restructuring techniques, such as cognitive behavioral therapy, can serve as effective tools in addressing these underlying processes by identifying and challenging the validity of automatic thoughts and core beliefs while countering the effects of validation and devaluation mechanisms.

## Common Patterns in Depressive Symptoms

1. Epidemiology of Depression and Cognitive Distortions:

When considering the relationship between depression and cognitive distortions, it becomes evident that distorted thinking patterns play a pivotal role in the development, maintenance, and exacerbation of depressive symptoms. Epidemiological studies have consistently highlighted the interplay between cognitive distortions and the prevalence of depression. These findings underscore the importance of addressing cognitive distortions in both prevention and treatment efforts. Epidemiological data also illuminate the diverse manifestations of depressive symptoms across different population subgroups. Variations in age, gender, socioeconomic status, and cultural background have been shown to influence the expression and experience of depression, shedding light on the nuanced nature of this multifaceted disorder. Furthermore, understanding the geographical distribution and temporal trends of depression provides valuable insights into the shifting landscape of mental health needs. Patterns of depression and cognitive distortions may vary across regions, and analyzing these variations can inform targeted interventions and resource allocation. Exploring the interaction between cognitive distortions and depression within specific demographic or cultural contexts can unveil unique challenges and opportunities for tailored interventions. Such insights allow for the development of more effective and culturally responsive strategies to address the burden of depression and its associated cognitive distortions.

2. Core Symptoms - Emotional and Cognitive Intersections:

The core symptoms of depression involve a complex interplay between emotional experiences and cognitive processes. Emotions such as sadness, hopelessness, and despair are integral components of depressive symptomatology, often intertwining with cognitive distortions to exacerbate the overall impact on an individual's mental health.

Emotional distress in depression is characterized by persistent feelings of sadness, emptiness, and profound sorrow. These emotions can significantly influence an individual's cognitive processing, leading to distorted perceptions of reality and an inability to experience positive emotions. The cognitive aspect of depression manifests through negative thought patterns, including pessimism, self-criticism, and a sense of helplessness. These cognitive distortions contribute to a skewed interpretation of events, further intensifying the emotional burden experienced by individuals with depression.

The intersection of emotions and cognition in depression often leads to rumination and recurrent negative thinking. Individuals may find themselves trapped in a cycle of distressing emotions and corresponding cognitive interpretations that reinforce the overarching sense of despair. As a result, their ability to engage in adaptive problem-solving and emotional regulation becomes severely compromised, perpetuating the cycle of depression.

The interaction between emotional and cognitive disturbances in depression can manifest in physical symptoms, such as fatigue, insomnia, and changes in appetite. These somatic manifestations further underscore the connections between the mind and body in the experience of depression, highlighting the holistic impact of the condition.

Understanding the emotional and cognitive intersections in depression is crucial for developing comprehensive intervention strategies that target both domains effectively. Integrating evidence-based approaches that address cognitive distortions, emotional dysregulation, and maladaptive coping mechanisms is essential for promoting recovery and long-term well-being in individuals experiencing depressive symptoms.

3. Anhedonia and Affective Blunting:

Anhedonia and affective blunting significantly impact an individual's emotional experience and overall quality of life. Anhedonia refers to the inability to experience pleasure or interest in previously enjoyable activities. It manifests as a pervasive sense of apathy and disconnection from once-rewarding pursuits, often leading to profound feelings of emptiness and despair. Affective blunting, on the other hand, involves a diminished range and intensity of emotional expression, with individuals experiencing a notable reduction in both positive and negative emotions. These two phenomena frequently co-occur in individuals with depression, exacerbating the severity and persistence of their symptoms. Understanding the nuanced nature of anhedonia and affective blunting is crucial for clinicians and researchers alike, as it informs targeted interventions and therapeutic approaches. Research suggests that anhedonia may arise from disruptions in the brain's reward circuitry, implicating dysregulation in dopamine signaling and neural processing of pleasurable stimuli. Moreover, affective blunting is thought to stem from alterations in emotional processing regions of the brain, resulting in compromised emotional reactivity and limited expressive range. Recognizing the interplay between these factors is paramount for developing tailored treatment plans that address the specific needs of individuals grappling with these debilitating symptoms. Furthermore, the impact of anhedonia and affective blunting extends beyond personal suffering, influencing social relationships, occupational functioning, and overall well-being. Individuals contending with these challenges often face significant barriers in seeking and sustaining social connections, as the diminished capacity for enjoyment and emotional engagement can lead to withdrawal and isolation. In professional settings, the blunting of affect may impede effective communication, interpersonal efficacy, and collaborative endeavors, further exacerbating the individual's distress. This interplay highlights the far-reaching implications of anhedonia and affective blunting, underscoring the imperative for comprehensive, multidimensional interventions that address the multifaceted repercussions of these symptoms.

4. Role of Negative Thinking Patterns in Depression:

Cognitive distortions, such as overgeneralization, magnification, and personalization, contribute to an individual's distorted perception of reality and self. These patterns of negative thinking often lead to a heightened sense of hopelessness, helplessness, and worthlessness, which are hallmark features of depression. When individuals consistently engage in negative thought processes, it can further exacerbate their emotional distress and hinder their ability to cope effectively with life stressors. Furthermore, these negative thinking patterns become ingrained in the individual's cognitive schema, leading to a self-reinforcing cycle of pessimism and despair. Acknowledging the pervasive nature of negative thinking in depression is paramount in developing effective therapeutic interventions. Therapists and mental health professionals need to work collaboratively with individuals experiencing depression to identify and challenge their negative thinking patterns. Cognitive restructuring techniques, such as cognitive-behavioral therapy, provide individuals with the tools to recognize and reframe maladaptive thoughts, ultimately shifting their cognitive perspective toward a more balanced and realistic view of themselves and the world. By addressing negative thinking patterns, therapists can empower individuals to develop adaptive coping strategies, enhance their resilience, and alleviate the burden of depressive symptoms. Additionally, fostering awareness of these negative thinking patterns within society is essential for reducing stigma and promoting understanding of the complex interplay between cognition and mood. Educating the public about the insidious nature of negative thinking in depression can facilitate earlier recognition of symptoms, encourage help-seeking behavior, and pave the way for compassionate support systems.

5. Chronic Stress Factors and Cognitive Responses:

Chronic stress is a prevalent factor in the development and perpetuation of depressive symptoms, with various cognitive responses contributing to this complex relationship. The experience of chronic stress can exert a profound impact on an individual's cognitive functioning, often leading to a heightened susceptibility to negative thinking patterns and distorted interpretations of events. In the context of cognitive distortions, chronic stress can act as a catalyst, amplifying the intensity and frequency of maladaptive cognitive responses. As individuals manage prolonged periods of stress, their cognitive resources may become depleted, making them more susceptible to cognitive bias and the amplification of negative interpretations of events. This process can lead to an exacerbation of depressive symptoms and contribute to the maintenance of dysfunctional cognitive patterns. Additionally, chronic stress may also influence the individual's cognitive flexibility and problem-solving abilities, leading to a narrowed focus on negative information and a reduced capacity to consider alternative perspectives or solutions. These shifts in cognitive processing can further entrench the individual in a cycle of pessimism and hopelessness, with the chronic activation of stress-related cognitive responses becoming deeply ingrained and resistant to change. Understanding the interplay between chronic stress factors and cognitive responses is essential for comprehensive interventions aimed at addressing depressive symptoms. Clinicians must recognize the impact of chronic stress on cognitive functioning and tailor therapeutic approaches to target both the stressors themselves and the accompanying maladaptive cognitive responses. By integrating stress reduction techniques, cognitive restructuring, and mindfulness-based interventions, mental health professionals can address the dynamics between chronic stress and cognitive responses, thereby offering individuals suffering from depression a comprehensive path towards recovery and resilience. It is crucial to acknowledge that addressing chronic stress factors and their cognitive correlates demands a multifaceted and holistic approach, encompassing not only cognitive-behavioral strategies but also systemic and environmental considerations.

6. Self-Perception and the Cycle of Pessimism:

Individuals grappling with depression often experience a distorted view of themselves, leading to a pervasive cycle of negative thought patterns and maladaptive behaviors. At the core of this phenomenon lies the concept of cognitive schemas – deeply ingrained belief systems that color an individual's interpretation of themselves and the world around them. These negative self-schemas can manifest as feelings of inadequacy, unworthiness, and a constant sense of failure, perpetuating a detrimental cycle of pessimistic thinking. Moreover, the persistent engagement with these negative self-beliefs reinforces maladaptive coping strategies and behavioral patterns, further reinforcing the cycle of pessimism.

The internal dialogue influenced by these negative self-perceptions often leads to a heightened sensitivity to perceived failures, rejections, and criticisms, amplifying feelings of despair and worthlessness. This self-reinforcing cycle intertwines with the individual's mood states, influencing their emotional well-being and overall functioning.

Recognizing and understanding the cycle of pessimism is crucial for effective intervention and treatment planning. Therapeutic approaches aimed at disrupting these negative self-schemas and promoting adaptive self-perceptions are integral in breaking the cycle of pessimism. By challenging cognitive distortions and facilitating a shift toward more balanced and realistic self-appraisals, individuals can begin to unravel the web of pessimism and gradually embrace a more optimistic outlook on themselves and their experiences.

7. The Feedback Loop Between Behavior and Mood States:

Individuals experiencing depressive symptoms often find themselves caught in a complex interplay between their behavior and mood states, each influencing the other in a continuous feedback loop. This dynamic relationship can perpetuate and exacerbate the experience of depression, significantly impacting an individual's daily functioning and overall well-being. Understanding this feedback loop is critical in devising effective interventions and treatment strategies for individuals struggling with depression.

Behavioral patterns have a profound impact on mood states, as they can either reinforce negative cognitive distortions or serve to challenge and alleviate them. Engaging in isolative behaviors, procrastination, or avoidance can heighten feelings of hopelessness and despair, further reinforcing the sense of being incapable or inadequate. On the other hand, active engagement in social activities, exercise, and pleasurable experiences can contribute to improved mood regulation and a sense of accomplishment, thereby disrupting the negative feedback loop.

Conversely, an individual's mood states significantly influence their behavioral choices. Persistent feelings of sadness or worthlessness may undermine motivation and energy levels, leading to withdrawal from activities that were once enjoyable or fulfilling. Additionally, heightened irritability or agitation can contribute to increased conflict in interpersonal relationships, consequently reinforcing negative self-perceptions and amplifying depressive symptoms.

Recognizing the bidirectional nature of this feedback loop is essential in developing targeted therapeutic interventions. Cognitive-behavioral approaches aim to interrupt this cycle by encouraging individuals to identify and modify maladaptive behavioral patterns while simultaneously challenging and restructuring negative thought processes. By addressing both behavior and mood states concurrently, these interventions strive to disrupt the reinforcement of depressive symptoms and foster adaptive coping strategies.

Interventions designed to target the feedback loop between behavior and mood states often incorporate elements of mindfulness-based practices and activity scheduling. Utilizing mindfulness techniques helps individuals develop greater awareness of their emotional and behavioral responses, fostering a more deliberate and intentional approach to managing their experiences. Similarly, structured activity scheduling assists in reinstating a sense of routine and accomplishment, bolstering positive reinforcement and countering the overwhelming inertia commonly associated with depression.

### Impact on Emotional Regulation and Behavior

1. Introduction:

Emotional regulation is a complex process involving both biological and psychological components that play crucial roles in modulating emotional responses. At the biological level, the brain's limbic system, particularly the amygdala and prefrontal cortex, is central to regulating emotions. The amygdala, often referred to as the brain's emotional center, plays a key role in detecting and responding to potential threats or rewarding stimuli. It processes emotional information and triggers corresponding physiological and behavioral reactions. On the other hand, the prefrontal cortex, known for its involvement in decision-making and cognitive control, helps regulate emotional responses by modulating the amygdala's activity and promoting reasoned thinking in situations of emotional arousal. This interplay between the amygdala and prefrontal cortex forms the foundation of emotional regulation at the neurological level. Additionally, neurotransmitters such as serotonin, dopamine, and norepinephrine also contribute to the modulation of emotional responses, influencing mood, arousal, and stress reactivity. Moving to the psychological aspect, factors such as early life experiences, learned behaviors, coping mechanisms, and cognitive appraisal all impact emotional regulation. For instance, individuals who have experienced supportive and nurturing environments in childhood may develop adaptive emotional regulation strategies, whereas those exposed to adverse experiences may struggle with dysregulated emotional responses. Moreover, the influence of cognitive appraisal, where individuals' interpretations and perceptions of events shape their emotional experiences, cannot be understated. Cognitive restructuring and reappraisal techniques are instrumental in altering emotional responses by challenging and modifying maladaptive thought patterns. Overall, the interplay between biological and psychological elements complexly shapes how individuals regulate their emotions, highlighting the multidimensional nature of emotional regulation.

2. Relationship Between Cognition and Emotion:

The relationship between cognition and emotion has been a subject of intense study within the fields of psychology, neuroscience, and psychiatry. Cognitive theories propose that emotions are influenced by how individuals perceive and interpret their internal and external experiences. Providing a comprehensive understanding of this relationship is crucial for elucidating the mechanisms underlying emotional dysregulation and cognitive distortions. Understanding the influence of cognition on emotion involves examining how individuals appraise and interpret situations, events, and stimuli. Cognitive appraisals, such as evaluating the significance of a potential stressor or determining the likelihood of success in a given task, directly influence the generation and intensity of emotional responses. Moreover, cognitive processes, including attention, memory, and reasoning, continually interact with emotional states, shaping perception and influencing decision-making. This bidirectional relationship is vital in comprehending the pervasive impact of cognitive distortions on emotional regulation and subsequent behavioral outcomes. Furthermore, recent advances in neuroimaging studies have provided valuable insights into the neural correlates of emotion-cognition interactions. Neuroscientific research has identified specific brain regions and functional networks involved in mediating the relationship between cognition and emotion, shedding light on the underlying neural mechanisms. An in-depth exploration of these neurological underpinnings is essential for elucidating the biological basis of emotional dysregulation and its association with cognitive distortions. Understanding the relationship between cognition and emotion is pivotal in addressing maladaptive emotional responses and dysfunctional behaviors manifested in various psychological disorders.

3. Cognitive Distortions and Emotional Dysregulation:

Cognitive distortions play a pivotal role in disrupting emotional regulation, leading to significant challenges in managing one's feelings and behavioral responses. These distortions, stemming from faulty thought processes, can generate an inaccurate perception of reality, exacerbating emotional dysregulation.

At the core of cognitive distortions lies a propensity to magnify negative events and minimize positive experiences, fostering a distorted emotional landscape. This distortion often manifests as an overwhelming sense of despair, hopelessness, and anxiety, impairing one's ability to regulate their emotions effectively. Moreover, the pervasive nature of these distortions can intensify emotional arousal, leading to impulsive and maladaptive behavioral responses. As individuals become ensnared in this cycle of distorted thinking and emotional dysregulation, the resultant behavioral manifestations further entrench the adverse effects on their psychological equilibrium.

Cognitive distortions, such as overgeneralization, personalization, and catastrophizing, can significantly disrupt emotional regulation by distorting perceptions of self, others, and the world. The incessant barrage of negative cognitive biases can foster a profound sense of vulnerability and threat, triggering heightened emotional reactivity and maladaptive coping mechanisms. Consequently, individuals may exhibit tendencies to engage in detrimental behaviors or withdrawal from social interactions, exacerbating the cycle of emotional dysregulation.

The interplay between cognitive distortions and emotional dysregulation underscores the profound impact on the individual's interpersonal relationships and overall functioning. These distortions can influence how individuals interpret and respond to cues from their environment, thereby shaping their behavioral repertoire. As a result, dysfunctional patterns of communication and interaction may emerge, hindering the establishment of healthy, supportive relationships and perpetuating the cycle of emotional turmoil.

4. Impact on Behavioral Responses:

When individuals experience distorted thinking patterns and struggle with regulating their emotions, it inevitably manifests in their behaviors, leading to a range of consequences and challenges. In many cases, individuals may exhibit avoidance behaviors, social withdrawal, or heightened irritability as they grapple with distorted perceptions of themselves and the world around them. Additionally, maladaptive coping strategies such as substance abuse or self-harm may arise as a result of emotional turmoil linked to distorted cognitions. These behavioral responses not only perpetuate the individual's distress but also contribute to interpersonal conflicts and impaired functioning in various domains of life, including work, relationships, and leisure activities. Furthermore, the interplay between cognitive distortions, emotional dysregulation, and behavioral responses often exacerbates the cycle of negative reinforcement, reinforcing dysfunctional patterns of thinking and feeling. For instance, individuals may engage in self-sabotaging behaviors that reinforce their negative beliefs, perpetuating a downward spiral of maladaptive responses. It is essential to recognize the connection between cognitive distortions, emotional dysregulation, and behavioral responses in order to effectively address these issues through targeted interventions. By comprehensively understanding the behavioral manifestations associated with cognitive distortions and emotional dysregulation, mental health professionals can tailor treatment approaches to mitigate the detrimental impact on individuals' lives. Moreover, an in-depth comprehension of the relationship between cognition, emotion, and behavior enables clinicians to identify specific triggers and antecedents that contribute to maladaptive responses, laying the groundwork for more precise and personalized therapeutic interventions.

5. Neuroscientific Perspectives on Emotion:

The neuroscientific study of emotion encompasses a multidisciplinary approach that integrates knowledge from neuroscience, psychology, and biology to elucidate the underlying mechanisms and pathways involved in emotional processing. At the core of this field is the exploration of neural structures, neurotransmitter systems, and functional connectivity patterns that underlie emotional experiences. One key aspect of neuroscientific research on emotion involves investigating the neural substrates associated with specific emotions, such as fear, joy, sadness, and anger. Advanced neuroimaging techniques, including functional magnetic resonance imaging and positron emission tomography, have provided valuable insights into the neural circuitry implicated in emotional responses.

Neuroscientific investigations have illuminated the interplay between the limbic system and cortical regions in mediating emotional regulation and processing. The amygdala, a pivotal structure within the limbic system, plays a central role in the rapid appraisal of emotional stimuli and the initiation of physiological and behavioral responses. Concurrently, the prefrontal cortex exerts regulatory control over emotional reactions through cognitive reappraisal and contextual evaluation of emotional stimuli. This dynamic interaction between subcortical and cortical regions underscores the complexity of emotion regulation and the susceptibility to cognitive distortions that may disrupt these processes.

The role of neurotransmitters, such as serotonin, dopamine, and norepinephrine, has been extensively studied in relation to emotional functioning. Neurotransmitter dysregulation has been implicated in various affective disorders, including depression, anxiety, and bipolar disorder, underscoring the critical involvement of neurochemistry in emotional states. Understanding the neurochemical underpinnings of emotions not only sheds light on the etiology of affective disturbances but also guides the development of pharmacological interventions targeting these neurotransmitter systems.

Advancements in neuroscientific methodologies have also led to the exploration of genetic and epigenetic influences on emotional reactivity and regulation. Research in molecular genetics has identified genes associated with emotional traits and susceptibilities to mood disorders, providing a comprehensive understanding of the genetic contributions to emotional phenotypes. Epigenetic modifications, including DNA methylation and histone acetylation, have been implicated in the modulation of gene expression related to emotional processing, offering promising avenues for therapeutic interventions targeting epigenetic mechanisms.

6. Affective Disorders:

Affective disorders encompass a wide array of mental health conditions characterized by disturbances in mood, emotions, and affect. Major Depressive Disorder (MDD) stands as one of the prevalent affective disorders, characterized by persistent feelings of sadness, hopelessness, and apathy. The contrasting periods of heightened energy and profound despondency hallmark bipolar disorder, contributing to its distinctive cyclical nature. Anxiety disorders encompass a varied spectrum, including generalized anxiety disorder (GAD), panic disorder, and social anxiety disorder, each presenting unique challenges in emotional regulation and stress response.

As we undertake the comparative analysis, it becomes evident that affective disorders share certain overlapping symptoms while also exhibiting distinct patterns that influence emotional reactivity and behavioral responses. Exploring the diagnostic criteria and clinical assessments employed in differentiating these disorders offers valuable insights into the diverse presentations observed in clinical practice. Moreover, understanding the neurobiological underpinnings and genetic predispositions associated with affective disorders contributes to a holistic appreciation of their impact on emotional regulation and behavioral dynamics.

The socio-cultural influences and environmental stressors intertwine with the manifestation and course of affective disorders, adding layers of complexity to the comparative landscape. By illuminating these interrelated factors, this comparative analysis intends to foster a deeper comprehension of the multifaceted nature of affective disorders, serving as a foundation for informed assessments and tailored interventions. Additionally, the section probes into the treatment modalities and therapeutic approaches tailored to address the specific symptomatology and functional impairments associated with various affective disorders, advocating for a personalized and integrated care framework.

7. Strategies for Enhancing Emotional Regulation:

Emotional regulation is a fundamental component of mental well-being and plays a pivotal role in our ability to manage life's challenges effectively. In this regard, it is pertinent to mention a series of crucial evidence-based strategies aimed at enhancing emotional regulation in individuals experiencing cognitive distortions and affective disorders.

- Mindfulness-Based Interventions: Mindfulness practices, such as meditation and focused attention exercises, have shown promising results in promoting emotional awareness and reducing reactivity to negative stimuli. By cultivating present-moment awareness, individuals can gain greater control over their emotional responses and develop resilience against cognitive distortions.

- Cognitive Restructuring Techniques: Cognitive behavioral therapy (CBT) offers powerful tools for challenging and restructuring maladaptive thought patterns. By identifying and modifying distorted beliefs, individuals can achieve greater emotional clarity and cognitive flexibility, leading to more adaptive behavioral responses.

- Emotion Regulation Skills Training: Equipping individuals with specific skills for recognizing, understanding, and modulating emotions forms the core of dialectical behavior therapy (DBT). This multifaceted approach encompasses emotion regulation, distress tolerance, interpersonal effectiveness, and mindfulness, providing a comprehensive framework for managing emotional dysregulation.

- Lifestyle Modification Strategies: Engaging in regular physical exercise, maintaining a balanced diet, and ensuring adequate sleep are integral aspects of emotional self-care. These lifestyle modifications contribute to neurobiological stability, thereby supporting effective emotional regulation and mitigating the impact of cognitive distortions on mood and behavior.

- Social Support and Connection: Cultivating meaningful social connections and seeking support from trusted individuals can serve as a buffer against the negative effects of cognitive distortions. Building a strong support network fosters emotional resilience and provides avenues for validation, empathy, and perspective taking, which are conducive to improved emotional regulation.

- Acceptance and Commitment Therapy (ACT): ACT emphasizes acceptance of internal experiences coupled with committed action toward values-driven goals. By fostering psychological flexibility and promoting mindful acceptance of thoughts and emotions, individuals can enhance their capacity for adaptive emotional regulation and pursue a purposeful life despite cognitive distortions.

Incorporating these strategies into clinical practice and personal wellness routines holds substantial promise for mitigating the detrimental effects of cognitive distortions on emotional regulation and behavioral responses. Moreover, ongoing research and innovation in this domain continue to expand the repertoire of interventions available.

8. Therapeutic Outcomes and Behavioral Adjustments:

As individuals engage in therapeutic interventions aimed at addressing cognitive distortions and enhancing emotional regulation, it is imperative to evaluate the potential outcomes and subsequent behavioral adjustments that may ensue. Therapeutic outcomes refer to the measurable changes in individuals' psychological well-being, cognitive processes, and behavioral patterns following the implementation of targeted interventions. These outcomes are pivotal in assessing the effectiveness of various therapeutic strategies. Additionally, identifying the behavioral adjustments resulting from improved emotional regulation allows for a comprehensive understanding of the holistic impact of therapeutic efforts. Through rigorous empirical research and clinical observation, a range of therapeutic outcomes and behavioral adjustments have been documented across diverse populations. One notable outcome pertains to the mitigation of maladaptive thought patterns and cognitive distortions. As individuals learn to recognize and challenge their distorted thinking, they often experience a reduction in negative affect and an enhanced ability to manage emotional responses. This, in turn, manifests in observable behavioral adjustments such as decreased avoidance behaviors, improved social interactions, and heightened decision-making capabilities. Furthermore, therapeutic interventions frequently contribute to a heightened sense of self-awareness and emotional insight, facilitating adaptive coping mechanisms and strengthened resilience in the face of adversity. Such outcomes not only mark the efficacy of intervention strategies but also highlight the impact of improved emotional regulation on individuals' daily functioning and overall well-being. An essential aspect of evaluating therapeutic outcomes and behavioral adjustments involves considering the sustained effects of interventions beyond the immediate treatment period. Follow-up assessments and longitudinal studies have shown that effective emotional regulation strategies can lead to enduring behavioral adjustments and sustained improvements in mental health outcomes. Consequently, individuals who have undergone successful therapeutic interventions often exhibit a greater capacity for problem-solving, increased motivation, and a more positive outlook on life. These enduring behavioral adjustments underscore the transformative potential of targeted interventions aimed at fostering emotional regulation and mitigating cognitive distortions.

## Diagnostic Tools and Identification Techniques

1. Clinical Interview Techniques and Protocols:

The clinical interview is a fundamental element of psychological assessment, allowing clinicians to gather valuable information directly from the client. The initial phase typically involves establishing rapport and building a therapeutic alliance with the client, creating a comfortable and safe environment for open communication. Clinicians use various questioning strategies, such as open-ended questions, structured interviews, and behavioral observations, to elicit detailed information about the client's thoughts, emotions, behaviors, and experiences. These techniques help in identifying cognitive distortions and assessing the client's overall mental state. Protocols for clinical interviews often include standardized assessments, ensuring consistent and systematic data collection. Additionally, professionals are trained to recognize non-verbal cues and cultural sensitivities, which can significantly impact the accuracy of the assessment. Understanding the nuances of verbal and non-verbal communication is crucial for effective interviews. Moreover, ethical considerations, confidentiality, and informed consent play pivotal roles in the implementation of these techniques, ensuring that the client's rights and well-being are upheld throughout the assessment process.

2. Utilization of Self-Report Inventories:

Self-report inventories typically involve standardized questionnaires or rating scales that allow individuals to express their thoughts, feelings, and behaviors in a structured format. By leveraging self-reports, clinicians can gain a more comprehensive understanding of a person's subjective experiences and internal states, which can be instrumental in identifying cognitive distortions, mood disturbances, and maladaptive thought patterns. When integrating self-report inventories into the assessment framework, it is essential to select measures with established reliability and validity, ensuring that the data collected accurately reflects the individual's psychological functioning. Additionally, careful consideration must be given to the specific constructs being assessed, tailoring the selection of inventories to target key areas such as depression, anxiety, irrational beliefs, or dysfunctional attitudes. Interpretation of self-report data requires a nuanced approach, taking into account potential response biases, cultural factors, and situational influences that may impact the individual's self-disclosure. Furthermore, integrating self-reports with information gathered from other assessment modalities, such as clinical interviews and behavioral observations, enhances the diagnostic utility and strengthens the overall clinical formulation. However, it is important to acknowledge limitations associated with self-report inventories, including tendencies for social desirability bias, response acquiescence, or difficulties in accurately recalling and reporting internal experiences.

Therefore, clinicians should approach the utilization of self-reports with a critical lens, supplementing questionnaire data with corroborating evidence from multiple sources to ensure a comprehensive and accurate assessment. As technology continues to evolve, there is a growing trend towards digital administration and scoring of self-report inventories, offering greater accessibility and streamlined data management. However, ethical considerations regarding data privacy, security, and the potential impact of technology on the therapeutic alliance must be carefully managed.

3. Behavioral Observation Methods:

Behavioral observation methods involve systematic recording and analysis of an individual's overt behavior in various settings, such as clinical environments, social interactions, or naturalistic settings. Through structured observations, professionals can gain valuable insights into the impact of cognitive distortions on an individual's behavioral responses and interpersonal dynamics.

One key aspect of behavioral observation methods is the use of standardized behavioral coding systems. These systems allow for the quantification and categorization of specific behaviors, providing a reliable framework for identifying patterns associated with cognitive distortions. By utilizing these standardized systems, clinicians can effectively capture and analyze behavioral data, which aids in the formulation of accurate assessments and tailored interventions.

Behavioral observation methods encompass direct monitoring of observable behaviors, including verbal and non-verbal expressions, emotional displays, and social interactions. This comprehensive approach enables clinicians to identify subtle cues and nuanced behavioral patterns that may align with specific cognitive distortions. Additionally, the incorporation of technology, such as video recordings or electronic monitoring devices, allows for more in-depth analysis and documentation of behavioral responses across diverse contexts.

Apart from the core observational practices, behavioral assessments often involve collaboration with relevant stakeholders, such as family members, caregivers, or peers. The input from these sources contributes to a holistic understanding of the individual's behavioral repertoire and assists in contextualizing observed behaviors within the individual's broader social environment.

Ethical considerations are paramount in conducting behavioral observations. Practitioners must ensure the privacy and dignity of the individual being observed while adhering to professional guidelines and legal regulations. Additionally, obtaining informed consent and maintaining confidentiality are central principles in ethical behavioral assessment practices.

4. Role of Neuropsychological Assessments:

Neuropsychological assessments play a crucial role in evaluating cognitive functions and identifying potential cognitive distortions. These assessments utilize a battery of standardized tests to measure various domains of cognitive functioning, including attention, memory, executive functions, language skills, visuospatial abilities, and motor dexterity. By examining these specific cognitive domains, clinicians can gain valuable insights into the underlying cognitive processes that may contribute to distorted thinking patterns in individuals. Furthermore, the results obtained from neuropsychological assessments can aid in differential diagnosis by distinguishing between cognitive distortions stemming from mood disorders and those associated with neurological conditions or injury. The comprehensive nature of these assessments allows for a thorough evaluation of an individual's cognitive strengths and weaknesses, providing a nuanced understanding of their cognitive profile. Moreover, the findings from neuropsychological assessments can inform treatment planning and intervention strategies tailored to address specific cognitive deficits. It is important to note that the interpretation of neuropsychological assessment results requires specialized expertise to ensure accurate analysis and meaningful application in the context of cognitive distortions. Clinicians must consider the influence of emotional factors on cognitive performance and interpret the findings within the broader psychological framework. Additionally, cultural and demographic variables should be taken into account to account for potential biases in cognitive assessment results. Integrating neuropsychological assessments with other diagnostic tools and identification techniques offers a more comprehensive understanding of an individual's cognitive functioning, thereby contributing to a holistic approach in addressing cognitive distortions. Overall, the role of neuropsychological assessments in the evaluation and identification of cognitive distortions is instrumental in guiding effective clinical interventions and promoting targeted cognitive remediation to alleviate the impact of distorted thinking patterns on individuals' emotional well-being and behavioral responses.

5. Interpreting Cognitive Test Results:

Cognitive tests offer valuable insights into an individual's cognitive functioning, including memory, attention, problem-solving abilities, and overall cognitive performance. It is essential to approach the interpretation of cognitive test results with a comprehensive understanding of the individual's unique background, cultural influences, and potential confounding factors.

A thorough analysis of cognitive test results involves examining performance across various cognitive domains. This includes assessing verbal and non-verbal reasoning, processing speed, working memory, and executive functions. Understanding the interplay between these cognitive domains can provide valuable information about an individual's cognitive strengths and weaknesses.

Interpreting cognitive test results necessitates consideration of age-appropriate norms and comparison with relevant population-based data. By contextualizing an individual's performance within a larger reference framework, clinicians can gain a deeper understanding of the significance of specific cognitive strengths or deficits. Additionally, it is crucial to recognize that test performance may be influenced by factors such as emotional state, motivation, and external distractions, all of which should be factored into the interpretation process.

In addition to considering the raw performance scores, interpreting cognitive test results involves analyzing patterns of responses and identifying any discrepancies that may indicate underlying cognitive distortions or atypical cognitive functioning. For instance, inconsistent performance across different cognitive tasks could signify potential areas of concern that warrant further exploration.

Qualitative observations such as the individual's approach to problem-solving, level of engagement during testing, and ability to adapt to changing task demands can offer valuable insights into their cognitive processing style and potential areas of difficulty. These qualitative aspects complement the quantitative test scores and contribute to a holistic interpretation of an individual's cognitive functioning.

It is imperative for clinicians to communicate the findings from cognitive test interpretation accurately and sensitively to the individuals being assessed, emphasizing the collaborative nature of the diagnostic process. Open dialogue and feedback allow for a more comprehensive understanding of the individual's cognitive strengths and limitations, fostering a foundation for personalized intervention strategies and supportive approaches.

6. Psychometric Evaluations:

Psychometric evaluations encompass a wide range of standardized tests and measures designed to quantify various aspects of cognition, personality, and emotional functioning. When incorporated effectively, psychometric evaluations can significantly contribute to the accurate diagnosis and formulation of targeted intervention strategies. One of the fundamental aspects of utilizing psychometric evaluations is the selection of appropriate assessment tools based on the specific clinical presentation and the underlying research-supported constructs. Understanding the psychometric properties of each test, including reliability, validity, and normative data, is crucial in ensuring the accuracy and interpretability of evaluation results. Moreover, it is imperative to consider cultural and linguistic factors when selecting and interpreting psychometric tests to minimize potential biases and enhance the validity of assessments across diverse populations. The administration and scoring of psychometric evaluations require adherence to standardized protocols to maintain consistency and reliability. Trained professionals should conduct these assessments in a controlled environment to optimize the quality of data obtained and minimize extraneous influences on test performance. Furthermore, ethical considerations regarding informed consent, confidentiality, and the utilization of assessment results should underpin the entire process of incorporating psychometric evaluations. Practitioners must communicate clearly with clients about the purpose, nature, and potential implications of these assessments to uphold ethical standards and ensure client understanding and cooperation. In addition to the quantitative data derived from psychometric evaluations, integration with qualitative information obtained through clinical interviews, behavioral observations, and collateral reports is essential in developing a comprehensive understanding of an individual's mental health status. This holistic approach facilitates a more nuanced and contextualized interpretation of assessment findings, leading to more accurate and clinically relevant diagnostic conclusions. Finally, ongoing professional development and training in the administration and interpretation of psychometric evaluations are indispensable for practitioners to maintain competence and expertise in employing these assessment tools effectively. Continuous refinement and updating of skills in utilizing psychometric evaluations are necessary to keep pace with advancements in the field and ensure the delivery of high-quality, evidence-based mental health care.

7. Challenges in Accurate Identification:

Accurately identifying cognitive distortions presents a multifaceted challenge due to the nature of human cognition and emotion. One primary challenge lies in the inherent subjectivity of human thought processes, making it difficult to uniformly categorize and label distorted thinking patterns. Additionally, individuals may not always manifest overt symptoms of cognitive distortions, which can further complicate accurate identification. Furthermore, the interconnectedness of cognitive distortions with other mental health conditions poses a significant challenge, as identifying and isolating specific cognitive distortions amidst a myriad of underlying issues demands skillful discernment. Cultural and linguistic barriers also contribute to the complexity of accurately identifying cognitive distortions, as different cultural contexts may influence how cognitive distortions manifest and are expressed. Moreover, the dynamic and fluctuating nature of cognitive distortions presents a continual challenge, as these distortions may morph or intensify over time, requiring ongoing vigilance and reassessment. Additionally, clinician bias and preconceptions may inadvertently influence the diagnostic process, potentially leading to misinterpretation or oversight of crucial indicators of cognitive distortions. The interplay between cognitive distortions and comorbid conditions necessitates a comprehensive and integrative approach to diagnosis, wherein clinicians must adeptly manage through layers of symptoms to pinpoint the specific cognitive distortions at play. Ethical considerations pose another critical challenge in accurately identifying cognitive distortions, as maintaining the autonomy and dignity of individuals while conducting assessments is paramount. Balancing the need for accurate diagnosis with the ethical obligation to minimize stigmatization and protect individual rights requires thoughtful consideration and skilled navigation. Finally, the evolving landscape of technology and its impact on human cognition introduces a novel challenge, as the digital age brings forth new forms of cognitive distortions that necessitate adaptation and awareness within diagnostic frameworks. Addressing these multifaceted challenges in accurate identification necessitates a nuanced and holistic approach that incorporates clinical expertise, cultural sensitivity, ethical mindfulness, and adaptability in the face of technological advancements.

8. Ethical Considerations in Diagnosis:

Ethical considerations are paramount in the diagnosis of cognitive distortions and related mental health conditions. Clinicians must adhere to strict ethical guidelines to ensure the well-being and autonomy of their clients while carrying out diagnostic procedures. One of the primary ethical considerations in diagnosis is confidentiality. Mental health professionals must maintain the privacy of their clients and safeguard their personal information from unauthorized access or disclosure. This involves securely storing client records, obtaining informed consent for sharing information with other healthcare providers, and only revealing confidential information when mandated by law or when necessary to prevent harm. Additionally, clinicians must remain vigilant about the potential misuse of diagnostic labels. It is crucial to approach diagnosis with cultural competence and sensitivity to avoid stigmatizing individuals based on their mental health conditions. Furthermore, it is essential to consider the implications of a diagnosis beyond the immediate treatment context. Ethical practitioners must weigh the potential impact of labeling on an individual's social relationships, employment opportunities, and self-perception. Competence and qualifications are also ethical imperatives in the diagnosis of cognitive distortions. Professionals should possess the appropriate training, knowledge, and expertise to conduct accurate and reliable assessments. It is unethical for individuals without proper credentials to administer diagnostic tests or offer clinical interpretations. Moreover, practitioners must strive for ongoing professional development to stay abreast of the latest advancements in assessment tools and diagnostic techniques. Informed consent is another pivotal ethical consideration in diagnosis. Clients have the right to be fully informed about the purpose, nature, and potential risks associated with the diagnostic procedures. Mental health professionals need to engage in transparent discussions with their clients, ensuring that they comprehend the assessment process and its implications. This includes providing clear explanations about the rationale behind specific evaluations, potential alternative approaches, and the expected outcomes of the diagnostic process. Finally, ethical practitioners prioritize the welfare and best interests of their clients throughout the diagnostic journey. They demonstrate empathy, respect, and nonjudgmental attitudes, fostering a therapeutic environment where clients feel comfortable disclosing their experiences and concerns.

9. Integration with Emotional and Behavioral Analysis:

Integrating cognitive assessment with emotional and behavioral analysis can offer a comprehensive understanding of an individual's psychological state. Emotional analysis involves examining the full spectrum of emotions experienced by the individual in response to various stimuli or situations. By exploring the intensity, frequency, and reactivity of these emotions, clinicians can gain insight into how cognitive distortions influence affective responses.

Behavioral analysis encompasses observing and evaluating an individual's overt actions, habits, and interpersonal interactions. By scrutinizing patterns of behavior, practitioners can identify maladaptive coping strategies or avoidance mechanisms rooted in distorted thinking patterns. Additionally, linking cognitive distortions with behavioral cues enables a more comprehensive assessment of the impact on an individual's daily functioning and social relationships.

Integrating cognitive assessment with emotional and behavioral analysis also allows for a more nuanced approach to intervention and treatment planning. Understanding how cognitive distortions contribute to specific emotional states or behavioral patterns can inform the development of targeted therapeutic techniques. For instance, cognitive-behavioral interventions can be tailored to address both the underlying distorted beliefs and the resulting emotional and behavioral disruptions.

This integrated approach facilitates the monitoring of treatment progress and the evaluation of therapeutic effectiveness. By continually assessing cognitive, emotional, and behavioral changes over the course of intervention, practitioners can gauge the extent to which cognitive restructuring and adaptive coping strategies are reshaping the individual's thought processes, emotional experiences, and behavioral responses.

**Intervention Strategies and Corrective Approaches**

1. Cognitive-Behavioral Therapy Techniques:

Cognitive-behavioral therapy (CBT) is a widely practiced psychotherapeutic approach that has proven effective in treating various mental health conditions. The core premise of CBT is rooted in the interplay between thoughts, emotions, and behaviors, emphasizing the reciprocal influence they have on each other. One of the key techniques employed in CBT is cognitive restructuring, which involves identifying and challenging maladaptive thought patterns. This process aims to replace negative or distorted thoughts with more balanced and rational ones.

Another fundamental aspect of CBT is behavioral activation, which focuses on identifying and modifying patterns of behavior that contribute to emotional distress. By engaging in structured activities that bring a sense of accomplishment or pleasure, individuals can counteract withdrawal and lethargy commonly associated with depression and other mood disorders.

CBT also utilizes systematic desensitization and exposure therapy to address anxiety-related concerns. These techniques involve gradually exposing individuals to feared or avoided situations while equipping them with coping strategies to manage their anxiety. Through repeated exposure, the aim is to reduce the intensity of anxiety responses and foster a sense of mastery over previously distressing stimuli.

On the other hand, CBT incorporates the use of homework assignments and self-monitoring tools to actively involve individuals in their therapeutic journey. These assignments may include tracking thoughts and emotions, practicing relaxation exercises, or implementing newly acquired skills in real-life scenarios.

In the context of cognitive-behavioral therapy, therapist-client collaboration plays a pivotal role. Therapists work to create a supportive and collaborative environment wherein individuals feel empowered to explore their internal experiences and develop adaptive strategies. This active involvement fosters a sense of agency and facilitates the transfer of skills from therapy sessions to daily life.

The effectiveness of CBT extends across diverse populations and psychological conditions, making it a versatile and valuable intervention. Research continues to demonstrate the efficacy of CBT in reducing symptom severity, preventing relapse, and improving overall functioning. As CBT evolves, efforts focus on tailoring interventions to individual needs, integrating cultural considerations, and exploring technological advancements to enhance treatment delivery.

2. Mindfulness and Acceptance-Based Strategies:

When addressing cognitive distortions, it is crucial to delve into mindfulness and acceptance-based strategies as they provide a valuable complement to traditional cognitive-behavioral techniques. Mindfulness, rooted in ancient contemplative practices, involves cultivating present-moment awareness and non-judgmental acceptance of one's experiences. By integrating mindfulness into therapy, individuals can develop a deeper understanding of their thought processes and emotional patterns, allowing them to respond more effectively to challenging situations. Acceptance-based strategies emphasize embracing difficult thoughts and feelings without attempting to change or suppress them. This approach encourages individuals to acknowledge the reality of their experiences and cultivate self-compassion, which is fundamental in combating cognitive distortions. Research has demonstrated that mindfulness and acceptance-based interventions have shown promising results in reducing depressive symptoms, anxiety, and stress. Understanding the underlying mechanisms of mindfulness and acceptance-based strategies will provide clinicians with effective tools to promote psychological well-being and enhance therapeutic outcomes.

3. Schema Modification and its Role:

As we know, schema modification plays a pivotal role in restructuring the deeply ingrained cognitive patterns and beliefs that contribute to cognitive distortions. These schemas, or core beliefs, form the foundation of an individual's perception of themselves, the world, and their future. They are often developed during early life experiences and can persist into adulthood, influencing thoughts, emotions, and behaviors. Understanding the influence of these schemas is crucial in addressing the root causes of cognitive distortions. Schema-focused interventions aim to identify and modify maladaptive schemas through a collaborative therapeutic process.

Therapists utilize various techniques such as cognitive restructuring, guided imagery, and experiential exercises to challenge and reframe negative schemas. By identifying specific triggering events or situations, individuals can work towards modifying their schemas and adopting healthier, more adaptive beliefs. Additionally, exploring the origins and maintenance of these schemas enables individuals to gain insight into how past experiences have shaped their current cognitive patterns. This heightened awareness serves as a catalyst for change, empowering individuals to challenge and revise their maladaptive cognitive structures.

Integrating schema modification within therapeutic interventions enhances the effectiveness of treatments for cognitive distortions and associated emotional distress. By targeting underlying core beliefs, therapists can help individuals break free from the cycle of recurrent negative thinking and self-defeating behaviors. In doing so, clients can develop a more balanced and nuanced perspective on themselves and their experiences, fostering resilience and improved emotional well-being.

Addressing schema modification in treatment plans involves tailoring interventions to the unique needs and circumstances of each individual. This personalized approach acknowledges the diverse nature of cognitive distortions and ensures that interventions are aligned with the individual's specific cognitive and emotional vulnerabilities. Through individualized strategies, therapists can effectively facilitate schema modification and guide clients towards long-lasting cognitive and emotional transformation.

4. Developing Personalized Treatment Plans:

A key aspect of modern mental health treatment involves the development of personalized and tailored treatment plans for individuals suffering from cognitive distortions and associated symptoms. One-size-fits-all approaches are often inadequate when addressing the complexity of distorted thinking patterns and emotional dysregulation experienced by different individuals.

To begin, a thorough assessment of the individual's cognitive distortions, emotional triggers, and behavioral responses is fundamental in shaping the treatment plan. This includes utilizing standardized assessment tools, conducting comprehensive interviews, and employing behavioral observations to gain a holistic understanding of the individual's cognitive processes and emotional regulatory mechanisms. By understanding the unique nuances of an individual's cognitive distortions, treatment can be customized to address specific patterns and triggers effectively.

An integrative approach that combines evidence-based interventions is crucial in developing personalized treatment plans. Cognitive-behavioral techniques, mindfulness practices, and schema-focused interventions can be seamlessly integrated based on the individual's needs and preferences. The emphasis is placed on tailoring therapeutic strategies to align with the individual's cognitive and emotional processing style, fostering an environment conducive to effective intervention.

Clinicians must also consider the individual's social and environmental context when devising personalized treatment plans. Understanding the impact of familial dynamics, work stressors, and societal influences is imperative in formulating interventions that account for the multifaceted nature of cognitive distortions. Additionally, collaborating with the individual in setting achievable goals and milestones empowers them to take an active role in their recovery journey, thereby enhancing the effectiveness of the treatment plan.

An integral component of personalized treatment plans involves regular reviews and adjustments based on the individual's progress and feedback. Flexibility in adapting the intervention strategies ensures that the treatment remains responsive to the evolving needs and challenges of the individual. Assessment tools and outcome measures serve as objective indicators for monitoring progress, guiding the iterative refinement of the treatment plan.

5. Leveraging Technology in Interventions:

The integration of technology in mental health interventions represents a significant advancement in the field, offering innovative solutions to enhance therapeutic outcomes. Various digital tools and platforms have emerged as valuable resources for both practitioners and individuals seeking support for cognitive distortions and related mental health challenges. Cognitive behavioral therapy apps, for instance, provide users with accessible and interactive exercises to identify and reframe negative thought patterns. These applications often feature guided self-help modules, mood tracking functionalities, and educational resources, enabling individuals to engage in structured interventions even outside traditional therapy sessions.

Virtual reality has also gained attention as a promising tool for addressing cognitive distortions by creating simulated environments where individuals can confront and manage distressing situations in a controlled setting. Through exposure therapy and immersive experiences, virtual reality technologies offer a unique avenue for desensitization and corrective learning, presenting opportunities for targeted interventions tailored to specific cognitive distortions.

Additionally, teletherapy and online counseling services have become increasingly prevalent, allowing individuals to access professional support remotely. The convenience and flexibility of virtual sessions enable more consistent engagement with therapy, reducing barriers related to geographical constraints and scheduling conflicts. Furthermore, internet-based interventions, such as web-based CBT programs, have demonstrated effectiveness in reaching diverse populations and delivering evidence-based treatments.

The utilization of machine learning algorithms and natural language processing is transforming the landscape of cognitive distortion interventions. These advancements contribute to personalized insights and adaptive interventions by analyzing extensive datasets to identify patterns in thought processes and tailor strategies accordingly. By harnessing these technologies, practitioners can refine treatment plans and optimize therapeutic approaches based on individualized profiles, ultimately enhancing the precision and efficacy of cognitive distortion interventions.

6. Resilience through Cognitive Training:

Building resilience through cognitive training is a critical aspect of intervention strategies aimed at addressing cognitive distortions and their impact on mental health. This approach focuses on enhancing an individual's ability to cope with stress, adversity, and emotional challenges by targeting specific cognitive patterns and thought processes.

Cognitive training programs are designed to strengthen cognitive skills such as attention, memory, problem-solving, and decision-making. By improving these foundational cognitive abilities, individuals can better regulate their emotions, manage intrusive thoughts, and develop more adaptive coping mechanisms.

One key aspect of resilience building through cognitive training is the cultivation of mental flexibility. This involves helping individuals recognize and challenge rigid or negative thinking patterns that contribute to distress. Through targeted exercises and interventions, individuals learn to reframe negative interpretations, broaden their perspective, and develop a more balanced and rational approach to interpreting life events.

Cognitive training for resilience often incorporates elements of mindfulness and self-awareness. Practicing mindfulness techniques allows individuals to cultivate present-moment awareness, reduce rumination, and increase psychological well-being. By integrating cognitive-behavioral principles with mindfulness practices, individuals can manage challenging situations with greater equanimity and composure.

Another important component of resilience-building cognitive training involves fostering a growth mindset. Individuals are encouraged to embrace a belief in their capacity for personal growth and adaptation. Through this perspective, setbacks and failures are reframed as opportunities for learning and development, leading to a more optimistic outlook and increased perseverance in the face of obstacles.

In addition to cognitive skill-building, resilience training often includes psychoeducation about cognitive distortions and their influence on emotional well-being. Through psychoeducational components, individuals gain insight into the nature of distorted thinking and its relationship to mood disturbances. This knowledge empowers individuals to recognize and address cognitive distortions, leading to greater self-efficacy and emotional regulation.

Effective implementation of cognitive training for resilience requires personalized treatment plans tailored to individual needs and goals. Clinicians and practitioners must consider factors such as cognitive strengths and weaknesses, specific mental health concerns, and the individual's readiness for change when developing and implementing these interventions.

7. The Effectiveness of Interventions:

Assessing the effectiveness of interventions in addressing cognitive distortions and related mental health challenges involves the systematic evaluation of the impact of therapeutic approaches on the thoughts, feelings, behaviors, and overall well-being of individuals. This process requires a comprehensive and multifaceted approach to ensure that the interventions are producing meaningful and sustainable changes.

One key element in assessing effectiveness is the use of standardized measurement tools and assessments. These instruments provide reliable and valid means of quantifying and evaluating symptoms, cognitions, and emotional states before, during, and after the intervention period. By comparing pre- and post-intervention scores, clinicians can gauge the magnitude of change and determine the extent to which the interventions have been successful in reducing cognitive distortions and associated distress.

Another critical component of effectiveness assessment involves tracking behavioral changes and adaptive coping strategies adopted by individuals post-intervention. For instance, monitoring the frequency and intensity of specific maladaptive behaviors or cognitive distortions can offer insights into the progress made during the therapeutic process. Qualitative data such as self-reports and diary entries can also provide a rich source of information regarding the individual's subjective experience and their perception of change over time.

The involvement of clients in self-assessment and feedback mechanisms is imperative. Establishing regular feedback sessions or using outcome measures that capture the client's perspective can enhance the validity and relevance of the effectiveness assessment. This participatory approach not only empowers the clients but also facilitates a collaborative dialogue between the clinician and the individual receiving treatment.

In addition to client-reported outcomes, it is essential to consider the objective indicators of functioning and well-being. This may include improvements in social and occupational functioning, reduced reliance on maladaptive coping strategies, and enhanced quality of life. Through careful observation and documentation, clinicians can gain a comprehensive understanding of the broader impact of interventions beyond symptom reduction.

Finally, longitudinal follow-up assessments are vital to evaluate the sustainability of treatment effects and the prevention of relapse. This long-term perspective allows for the examination of enduring changes in cognitive patterns and emotional regulation, thereby providing valuable insights into the lasting impact of interventions on individuals' mental health.

8. Collaborative Approaches with Healthcare Providers:

Effective collaboration between mental health professionals and healthcare providers is essential for providing comprehensive and integrated care to individuals with cognitive distortions and related mental health issues. This collaborative approach involves a multidisciplinary team of professionals, including psychiatrists, psychologists, social workers, and primary care physicians, working together to address the complex needs of the patient.

Communication and coordination play a pivotal role in collaborative care. Regular and clear communication among team members ensures that relevant information regarding the patient's diagnosis, treatment plan, and progress is shared effectively. It is crucial for healthcare providers to have access to the patient's mental health records and assessments to make informed decisions about their overall care.

Collaborative approaches focus on holistic well-being, recognizing that mental health conditions can often be intertwined with physical health challenges. Psychiatric medications may interact with other prescribed medications, requiring close monitoring and coordination between mental health providers and primary care physicians to mitigate potential risks and optimize treatment outcomes.

In collaborative care models, healthcare providers engage in ongoing discussions with mental health professionals to identify potential barriers to treatment adherence, respond to emergent symptoms, and make adjustments to the treatment plan as necessary. Integrating behavioral health into primary care settings through consultation-liaison services enables early detection and intervention for individuals at risk of developing cognitive distortions or experiencing related mental health concerns.

Collaborative approaches extend to supporting patients during transitional phases of care, such as from inpatient psychiatric facilities to outpatient settings or during the transition from pediatric to adult care. This continuity of care promotes seamless and coordinated support, reducing the likelihood of treatment gaps and enhancing long-term outcomes for individuals with cognitive distortions.

Ethical considerations are paramount in collaborative care, ensuring that all professionals uphold confidentiality, respect autonomy, and prioritize the best interests of the patient. When collaborating with healthcare providers, mental health professionals adhere to regulatory standards and ethical guidelines, maintaining professional boundaries while working towards a unified goal of optimizing patient care.

9. Ethical Considerations in Therapeutic Practices:

Ethical guidelines serve as a compass that directs the actions and decisions of mental health professionals, ensuring the welfare and rights of clients are consistently upheld. In the context of therapeutic practices, several key ethical considerations must be carefully addressed to promote trust, respect, and positive outcomes for clients.

Confidentiality stands as one of the foundational ethical principles in therapeutic practices. Mental health professionals are entrusted with sensitive information by their clients, and it is crucial to maintain confidentiality to build a safe and trusting therapeutic environment. Understanding the boundaries and limitations of confidentiality, including circumstances where disclosure may be necessary (such as mandated reporting of harm or danger), is essential for ethical practice.

Informed consent is another critical aspect of ethical therapeutic practices. Prior to commencing any intervention or treatment, clients have the right to be informed about the nature of the treatment, its potential risks and benefits, and any available alternatives. This ensures that individuals are empowered to make autonomous decisions about their care, contributing to a collaborative and respectful therapeutic relationship.

Professional competence and integrity form the bedrock of ethical therapeutic practices. Mental health professionals must possess the knowledge, skills, and experience required to provide competent care to their clients. Additionally, they are obligated to engage in ongoing professional development and engage only in practices that align with evidence-based standards. Upholding integrity involves being truthful, avoiding conflicts of interest, and adhering to professional standards of conduct at all times.

The principle of beneficence emphasizes the obligation of mental health professionals to act in the best interests of their clients, striving to maximize benefits and minimize harm. This ethical consideration underscores the importance of utilizing interventions that are likely to result in positive outcomes while avoiding practices that may cause unnecessary distress or harm. Similarly, the principle of nonmaleficence dictates the responsibility of professionals to do no harm, emphasizing the need to carefully assess the potential risks of interventions and strive to do everything possible to prevent harm to clients.

Cultural competence and sensitivity are integral ethical considerations in therapeutic practices, particularly in our increasingly diverse society. Mental health professionals must recognize and respect the influences of culture, race, ethnicity, and other factors on an individual's mental health and wellbeing. By integrating cultural competence into therapeutic approaches, professionals can ensure that interventions are respectful, inclusive, and relevant to clients' unique cultural backgrounds and belief systems.

Maintaining ethical boundaries in therapeutic relationships is also crucial. Establishing clear boundaries and roles, such as maintaining a professional demeanor, avoiding dual relationships, and setting appropriate communication norms, fosters a safe and healthy therapeutic environment. Additionally, ethical considerations extend to issues such as fees, professional accountability, and boundaries of competence, all of which are essential for ensuring the professionalism and integrity of therapeutic practices.

Ultimately, adherence to ethical considerations in therapeutic practices not only upholds the dignity and rights of clients but also contributes to the ongoing progress and credibility of the mental health profession as a whole. By continuously prioritizing ethical principles, mental health professionals can foster a climate of trust, safety, and respect, laying the groundwork for meaningful and effective therapeutic experiences for those seeking support for their mental and emotional wellbeing.

## Long-Term Implications for Mental Health Outcomes

1. Introduction to Cognitive Distortion's Enduring Effects:

The enduring effects of cognitive distortions encompass a broad spectrum of psychological and behavioral outcomes. These distortions can contribute to the development and perpetuation of various mental health conditions, including anxiety disorders, depression, and other mood disturbances. Moreover, individuals experiencing cognitive distortions may also exhibit impaired coping mechanisms, maladaptive behaviors, and interpersonal difficulties over an extended period.

The enduring effects of cognitive distortions extend beyond the individual level and can impact social and occupational functioning. Research suggests that individuals grappling with persistent cognitive distortions may face challenges in maintaining healthy relationships, pursuing educational or career goals, and participating in community activities. As such, the enduring effects of cognitive distortions have far-reaching implications that warrant careful consideration and intervention.

Examining the enduring effects of cognitive distortions also involves exploring their influence on key aspects of daily functioning. Individuals affected by cognitive distortions may experience disruptions in their attention, concentration, and decision-making processes, ultimately affecting their ability to engage effectively in personal and professional pursuits. Additionally, cognitive distortions can undermine individuals' self-esteem, self-efficacy, and resilience, diminishing their capacity to manage challenges and setbacks in a constructive manner.

It is imperative to recognize that the enduring effects of cognitive distortions are not immutable. By implementing targeted interventions, such as cognitive-behavioral therapy and mindfulness-based approaches, mental health professionals can help individuals alleviate the entrenched impact of cognitive distortions and foster adaptive thought patterns and behaviors. Moreover, raising awareness and providing psychoeducation about cognitive distortions' enduring effects within communities and support networks can facilitate early recognition and prompt intervention, thereby promoting long-term mental well-being.

2. Baseline Mental Health Indicators:

Assessing baseline mental health indicators involves the comprehensive evaluation of various psychological, emotional, and behavioral factors to establish a starting point for assessing changes over time. It often begins with a thorough review of the individual's mental health history, including any previous diagnoses, treatments, and personal experiences. Additionally, standardized assessment tools and measures, such as structured interviews and validated questionnaires, are utilized to gather quantitative and qualitative data regarding the individual's current mental state. These assessments provide valuable insights into the presence and severity of symptoms related to cognitive distortions, including patterns of negative thinking, maladaptive behaviors, and disturbances in emotional regulation. Furthermore, baseline assessments also encompass an exploration of the individual's social support network, coping strategies, and overall quality of life. By considering these multifaceted dimensions, clinicians can obtain a holistic understanding of the individual's mental health status at a specific point in time. When evaluating baseline mental health indicators, it is imperative to consider potential confounding variables, such as comorbid conditions, environmental stressors, and socioeconomic factors, that may influence the individual's psychological well-being. The integration of interdisciplinary perspectives, including psychiatry, psychology, and social work, ensures a comprehensive assessment that accounts for the complex interplay of biological, psychological, and social determinants of mental health. Moreover, the use of culturally sensitive and context-specific assessment approaches is fundamental in recognizing and respecting the diversity of human experiences. Through this nuanced evaluation, practitioners can identify areas of strength and resilience in the individual, as well as areas of vulnerability and potential deterioration. This knowledge forms the foundation for monitoring and measuring changes in mental health outcomes over time, guiding the development of personalized interventions, and facilitating collaborative decision-making with the individual in promoting their long-term well-being and recovery.

3. Impacts on Cognitive Function over Time:

Studies have consistently shown that individuals struggling with cognitive distortions are more likely to experience difficulties in various cognitive domains. One of the key areas affected is memory. Persistent negative thinking and rumination can impede memory encoding and retrieval processes, leading to reduced cognitive flexibility and efficiency. Additionally, cognitive distortions can hamper executive functions such as problem-solving, decision-making, and attention regulation, thereby influencing overall cognitive performance. Furthermore, the chronic activation of distorted thinking patterns can contribute to a decline in mental agility and adaptability, making it challenging for individuals to cope with novel or uncertain situations. Over time, these cognitive impairments can impact an individual's ability to engage in productive and fulfilling activities, ultimately affecting their overall quality of life. It is imperative to acknowledge the long-term consequences of cognitive distortions on cognitive function and emphasize the importance of early intervention and ongoing support to mitigate these detrimental effects.

4. Behavioral and Emotional Consequences:

In examining behavioral consequences, it becomes evident that cognitive distortions can significantly influence an individual's decision-making processes, often leading to maladaptive behaviors. These distorted thought patterns may result in avoidance behaviors, self-isolation, or even impulsive actions detrimental to one's well-being. Furthermore, recurrent negative thought patterns associated with cognitive distortions might exacerbate the likelihood of engaging in harmful coping mechanisms such as substance abuse or aggressive behavior.

The emotional ramifications of cognitive distortions cannot be understated. Pervasive negative thinking can contribute to the development of persistent feelings of sadness, hopelessness, and worthlessness. These emotions may further manifest as heightened anxiety, irritability, or a pervasive sense of despair. The prolonged influence of cognitive distortions on emotional states can also impair an individual's ability to experience joy, engage in meaningful relationships, and maintain a positive outlook on life.

Importantly, these behavioral and emotional consequences can become entrenched over time, reinforcing and perpetuating the cycle of cognitive distortions. They may lead to a decreased quality of life, hindered social functioning, and compromised mental well-being. It is crucial for mental health professionals and individuals themselves to recognize and address these consequences proactively.

Identifying, understanding, and effectively managing the behavioral and emotional repercussions of cognitive distortions is integral to promoting holistic recovery and fostering resilience. By acknowledging the connection between distorted thoughts, emotions, and behaviors, individuals can develop coping strategies, seek appropriate support, and ultimately work towards reclaiming agency over their lives.

5. Longitudinal Studies and Findings:

Longitudinal studies are essential in unraveling the tapestry of cognitive distortions, offering valuable insights into how these distorted thought patterns evolve over time and the subsequent impacts on an individual's mental well-being. These longitudinal studies often span years or even decades, enabling researchers to observe the trajectory of cognitive distortions and their correlation with various mental health outcomes. Such in-depth investigations provide a comprehensive understanding of the persistence and fluctuation of cognitive distortions, shedding light on their influence on individuals' psychological states.

One pivotal aspect illuminated by longitudinal studies is the identification of potential trajectories of cognitive distortions and their association with specific mental health conditions. Through meticulous data collection and analysis, researchers have discerned distinct pathways of cognitive distortions, ranging from relatively stable patterns to those characterized by fluctuations and exacerbations. These findings contribute to the development of tailored intervention strategies that cater to the nuances of each trajectory, thereby fostering more effective and personalized approaches to treatment.

Longitudinal studies allow for the exploration of the interplay between cognitive distortions and other psychosocial variables, unveiling complex relationships that unfold over extended periods. By examining how cognitive distortions interact with factors such as social support, life events, and coping mechanisms, researchers can ascertain the compounding or mitigating influences that shape individuals' long-term mental health outcomes.

These in-depth investigations enable the identification of critical turning points or pivotal events that may significantly impact the course of cognitive distortions and, subsequently, mental health trajectories. Whether it be the onset of a stressor, the implementation of a therapeutic intervention, or the occurrence of a major life transition, longitudinal studies unveil the dynamic nature of cognitive distortions and the momentous factors that shape their developmental pathways.

The revelations gleaned from longitudinal studies not only contribute to the refinement of existing theoretical models but also propel forward the advancement of predictive models that forecast long-term mental health outcomes based on the trajectory of cognitive distortions. These predictive models serve as invaluable tools in clinical practice, empowering mental health professionals to anticipate and prevent adverse outcomes, as well as tailor interventions based on projected trajectories of cognitive distortions.

6. Risk Factors and Predictive Models:

The examination of risk factors and the development of predictive models has been a critical area of research in understanding the long-term implications of cognitive distortions on mental health outcomes. By identifying the specific variables and conditions that increase the likelihood of sustained negative effects, mental health professionals can better tailor interventions and preventive strategies.

Numerous studies have outlined a range of risk factors associated with persistent cognitive distortions, including but not limited to early childhood adversity, trauma exposure, family history of mental illness, socioeconomic disparities, chronic stress, and lack of social support. These factors act as significant contributors to the maintenance and exacerbation of distorted thinking patterns over time.

In addition to identifying individual risk factors, the construction of predictive models has played a pivotal role in anticipating the trajectories of mental health outcomes. The integration of demographic, psychological, and environmental variables into these models has allowed for the development of algorithms that offer insights into the potential long-term consequences of untreated cognitive distortions. Leveraging advanced statistical methods such as machine learning and longitudinal data analysis, these models provide valuable information for early intervention and resource allocation.

Researchers have delved into investigating the interaction between risk factors and protective factors, acknowledging the complex interplay between vulnerability and resilience. Understanding how protective factors, such as coping mechanisms, social support networks, and access to mental health services, can mitigate the impact of risk factors is integral in shaping targeted and holistic approaches to long-term mental health management.

As we continue to refine our understanding of risk factors and predictive models, it is imperative to acknowledge the intersectionality of these influences across diverse populations. Cultural, ethnic, and contextual variations may shape the manifestation and persistence of cognitive distortions, necessitating culturally sensitive and inclusive approaches to risk assessment and prediction. The ongoing integration of multidisciplinary perspectives and collaborative research endeavors will further enhance our ability to identify and address the multifaceted risk landscape surrounding cognitive distortions and mental health outcomes.

# THE ROLE OF SCHEMA IN SUSTAINING DEPRESSIVE PATTERNS

## Theoretical Underpinnings and Origins of Schema Theory

1. Foundational Theories in Cognitive Psychology:

The early 20th century saw a fundamental shift in psychological discourse, moving away from behaviorism and towards the exploration of internal mental processes. This paradigmatic shift paved the way for foundational theories in cognitive psychology, setting the stage for the eventual conceptualization of schemas as vital cognitive structures.

Cognitive psychology has played a pivotal role in shaping our understanding of human cognition and behavior. Dating back to the mid-20th century, this field has witnessed the emergence of influential theories that have significantly contributed to the development of schema theory. One such foundational theory is the influential work of Jean Piaget, whose pioneering research on cognitive development laid the groundwork for understanding how individuals acquire and organize information. Piaget's constructivist approach emphasized the active role of individuals in constructing their understanding of the world, thus paving the way for the notion of mental frameworks or schemas.

Another cornerstone in cognitive psychology is the information processing approach, which views the mind as a complex information-processing system akin to a computer. This theoretical framework, championed by researchers such as George Miller and Ulric Neisser, elucidated how individuals encode, process, store, and retrieve information. Notably, this perspective underscores the importance of cognitive structures and processes, aligning closely with the concept of schemas as fundamental units of knowledge that influence perception and interpretation.

The social cognitive theory, as advanced by Albert Bandura, contributed a socio-cognitive perspective to the understanding of human behavior. Bandura's emphasis on observational learning, self-efficacy, and the reciprocal interaction between individuals and their environment further enriched the conceptualization of cognitive processes, underscoring the role of schemas in mediating social learning and adaptive behaviors.

Equally consequential is the work of Lev Vygotsky, whose sociocultural theory shed light on the dynamic interplay between cultural influences and cognitive development. Vygotsky's zone of proximal development and the concept of scaffolding underscored the role of social interactions and cultural tools in shaping cognitive processes, accentuating the interconnectedness of individual schemas with external sociocultural factors.

Lastly, the groundbreaking works of cognitive psychologists such as Jerome Bruner and Ulric Neisser have significantly influenced the formation and evolution of schema theory. Bruner's constructivist theory and the notion of cognitive scaffolding have provided valuable insights into how individuals actively build their understanding through interaction with their environment, while Neisser's seminal contributions to ecological psychology have underscored the significance of environmental context in shaping cognitive representations and mental frameworks. These foundational theories in cognitive psychology collectively set the stage for an in-depth exploration of schema theory, bridging the gap between cognitive processes and the construction of internalized cognitive structures.

2. Influential Contributors and Key Works:

The evolution and consolidation of schema theory in the domain of psychological research have been significantly shaped by the contributions of several influential figures and their seminal works. As previously stated, one key figure in this arena is Aaron Beck, whose pioneering work in cognitive therapy laid the groundwork for the identification and exploration of dysfunctional schemas in individuals with depression and other psychological disorders. Beck's development of the concept of cognitive schemas provided a pivotal bridge between cognition and affect, offering a new lens through which to comprehend and address maladaptive thought patterns.

On the other hand, the prolific writings of Jeffrey Young have played a fundamental role in elaborating on the architecture of early maladaptive schemas and their influence on emotional and behavioral responses. Young's delineation of distinct schema domains and modes has greatly enriched the therapeutic interventions targeting these deep-seated cognitive structures. His collaborative efforts in formulating the Schema Therapy approach have garnered widespread recognition and adoption in clinical practice, fostering a paradigm shift in the treatment of personality disorders and chronic mental health conditions.

Another luminary in the field, Arnold A. Lazarus, contributed significantly to the integration of psychoanalytic principles with cognitively oriented techniques, thereby paving the way for an integrative model that acknowledges the multifaceted nature of human experience. By emphasizing the interplay between early experiences and current cognitive processes, Lazarus accentuated the relevance of schemas in perpetuating intrapsychic conflicts and maladaptive coping mechanisms. His oeuvre reflects a harmonious fusion of cognitive restructuring and psychodynamic exploration, echoing the harmony observed within the sphere of schema theory.

Additionally, the groundbreaking research conducted by Marsha M. Linehan deserves recognition for its transformative impact on schema-focused interventions, particularly in the context of borderline personality disorder. Linehan's dialectical behavior therapy (DBT) has elucidated the profound linkages between emotion dysregulation and schema-related vulnerabilities, outlining innovative strategies to promote emotional resilience and adaptive functioning in individuals grappling with pervasive maladaptive schemas. Her comprehensive elucidation of the dialectical worldview has informed the compassionate and pragmatic management of complex developmental trauma and chronic emotional distress.

3. The Intersection of Schema Theory and Psychoanalysis:

The convergence of schema theory and psychoanalysis has sparked profound scholarly discourse, enriching our comprehension of the underpinnings of human experience. Sigmund Freud's pioneering work serves as a cornerstone for the integration of psychoanalytic principles into schema theory. The emphasis on unconscious processes, early childhood experiences, and the impact of past traumas aligns closely with the domain of maladaptive schemas and their origins. Furthermore, the incorporation of defense mechanisms within psychoanalytic frameworks resonates with the notion of cognitive distortions, shedding light on adaptive and maladaptive coping strategies. Moreover, while psychoanalysis traditionally focuses on intrapsychic conflicts, schema theory expands this perspective by examining the interplay between internal schemas and external triggers in shaping an individual's emotional and cognitive responses. This amalgamation underscores the complementary nature of these constructs in elucidating the multifaceted nature of psychopathology. Concurrently, the symbiotic relationship between schema theory and psychoanalysis catalyzes therapeutic innovations, fostering the evolution of integrative approaches that amalgamate cognitive restructuring techniques with insight-oriented interventions. As such, the interconnection of these theoretical frameworks paves the way for comprehensive treatment modalities that holistically address the tapestry of an individual's psychological landscape.

4. Schema Theory Within Behavioral Frameworks:

Behavioral psychology, more commonly known as behaviorism, postulates that behaviors are learned through conditioning and that environmental factors are significant determinants of an individual's cognitive and emotional processes. This fundamental premise forms the backdrop for analyzing how schema theory intertwines with behavioral paradigms. When examining schema theory within behavioral frameworks, one encounters the influential work of prominent behaviorists such as B.F. Skinner and Albert Bandura. Skinner, a proponent of operant conditioning, explored how reinforcement and punishment mechanisms contribute to the formation and perpetuation of cognitive structures. His emphasis on observable behaviors and environmental contingencies provides a fitting context to examine the acquisition and maintenance of schemas within behavioral psychology. Moreover, Bandura's social learning theory underscores the significance of observational learning and modeling in schema development. By scrutinizing the interplay between cognitive schemas and behavioral manifestations, Bandura's research opens avenues to explore the bidirectional relationship between cognitive processes and external experiences.

The application of behavioral experiments to elucidate schema activation and modification enriches our comprehension of the behavioral underpinnings of schema theory. Behavioral experiments offer a methodological approach to investigate how specific stimuli and responses influence schema-related cognitions and emotional states. These experiments not only contribute to understanding the core tenets of behavioral psychology but also shed light on the nuanced ways in which individuals assimilate and accommodate schemas based on environmental cues and behavioral patterns. Delving into the sphere of behavioral frameworks also entails a comprehensive examination of behavioral interventions targeting maladaptive schemas. Cognitive-behavioral therapies, grounded in behavioral principles, have demonstrated efficacy in addressing dysfunctional schemas through structured interventions that focus on modifying behaviors and cognitions. Exploring these therapeutic modalities within the framework of schema theory enriches our understanding of how behavioral mechanisms can be harnessed to restructure maladaptive thought patterns.

5. Critiques and Controversies in Early Developments:

As schema theory gained traction within the field of psychology, it also encountered various critiques and controversies, offering valuable insights into its early developments. One of the primary criticisms centered on the subjective nature of schema formation and activation, with skeptics questioning the universality and generalizability of schema models across diverse populations. Additionally, concerns arose regarding the potential oversimplification of complex cognitive processes within the existing framework, raising doubts about the comprehensive nature of schema theory. Moreover, the deterministic implications of early schema theories faced scrutiny, as critics argued that these perspectives may overlook individual agency and variability, potentially undermining the nuance of human cognition.

Controversies surrounding the empirical validation of schemas also emerged, sparking debates about the reliability and validity of measures used to assess schema constructs. Skeptics highlighted the challenges associated with capturing the multidimensional facets of schemas through traditional research methodologies, urging for a more nuanced approach to empirical investigations. Furthermore, ethical considerations surfaced regarding the potential stigmatization of individuals based on predefined schema categories, foregrounding the need for sensitivity and ethical rigor in schema-related studies.

Amidst these critiques and controversies, the evolution of schema theory unfolded, prompting scholars to recalibrate their approaches and refine the conceptual foundations of schemas. These early debates catalyzed a shift towards integrative frameworks that acknowledged the complexity and individual differences in schema development and activation. The dynamism inherent in cognitive processes received augmented attention, steering the field towards more holistic and inclusive conceptualizations of schemas. Moreover, the emphasis on empirical rigor led to methodological advancements that aimed to capture the dynamic interplay between cognitive processes and environmental influences, enriching the empirical landscape of schema research.

6. Emergence of Empirical Studies on Schemas:

With the development of schema theory in psychology, the emergence of empirical studies marked a pivotal shift in the understanding and validation of the theoretical constructs. Empirical investigations aimed to explore the cognitive processes and behavioral manifestations associated with schemas across diverse populations and clinical presentations. These studies sought to provide rigorous evidence for the existence of maladaptive schemas, their underlying mechanisms, and their implications for mental health and well-being.

Pioneering researchers in the field recognized the need to bridge the gap between theoretical conjecture and empirical validation. Their efforts led to the formulation of systematic methodologies to measure and assess schemas, laying the groundwork for a robust empirical foundation. Through a combination of survey instruments, clinical interviews, and experimental paradigms, researchers endeavored to capture the nuances of schema activation, maintenance, and modification in various contexts.

Empirical studies not only confirmed the presence of maladaptive schemas in individuals experiencing depression, anxiety, and personality disorders but also shed light on the interplay between cognitive schemas and emotional regulation. These investigations provided invaluable insights into the cognitive-affective components of schemas, elucidating how dysfunctional schemas contribute to the perpetuation of negative affect and psychological distress. Moreover, empirical research delved into the developmental trajectories of schemas, uncovering their origins in childhood experiences and their influence on adult functioning.

The emergence of empirical studies on schemas also facilitated the identification of specific cognitive distortions aligned with maladaptive schemas. By discerning the cognitive biases and irrational beliefs underpinning dysfunctional schemas, researchers could delineate targeted interventions aimed at restructuring cognitive processes and ameliorating psychological symptoms. Additionally, empirical findings underscored the dynamic nature of schemas, highlighting their susceptibility to modification through therapeutic interventions and cognitive restructuring techniques.

Empirical endeavors engendered a greater understanding of the relational and interpersonal dimensions of schemas, unveiling the ways in which early relational patterns and attachment styles shape individuals' schema repertoire. These studies illuminated the reciprocal influence between interpersonal experiences and the formation of cognitive schemas, offering implications for relational therapies and systemic interventions within a clinical framework.

As empirical studies burgeoned, they not only validated the tenets of schema theory but also catalyzed its integration into evidence-based practice. The empirical validation of schemas as transdiagnostic constructs with relevance across diverse psychological presentations fostered interdisciplinary collaborations and enriched the repertoire of interventions targeting cognitive schemas within the sphere of clinical psychology and psychotherapy.

7. Role of Neuroscience in Understanding Schema Origins:

Neuroscience has significantly advanced our understanding of the origins of schemas, shedding light on the neural underpinnings of cognitive processes that contribute to schema formation. Research in this field has revealed complex connections between brain structures and the development, maintenance, and activation of schemas. The neural basis of schema formation is rooted in the plasticity of the brain, particularly in regions associated with memory, emotion regulation, and cognitive processing.

Studies utilizing neuroimaging techniques such as functional magnetic resonance imaging have provided valuable insights into how different brain regions are involved in encoding, storing, and retrieving information relevant to schema-relevant experiences. For example, the hippocampus, a crucial structure for memory consolidation, has been implicated in the formation of schemas by integrating new information into existing cognitive frameworks. Furthermore, the amygdala, known for its role in emotional processing, has been linked to the formation and modulation of affect-laden schemas, highlighting the intertwining of cognitive and emotional elements in schema development.

Advancements in neuroscience have also elucidated the impact of early life experiences on brain development and the subsequent shaping of schemas. Adverse childhood experiences, trauma, and chronic stress have been shown to exert lasting effects on the structural and functional connectivity of neural circuits involved in schema processing. These alterations can manifest as heightened reactivity to schema-related triggers and maladaptive cognitive patterns in adulthood, underscoring the interplay between neurobiological factors and the genesis of dysfunctional schemas.

Research exploring the neurochemical substrates of schema-related processes has underscored the influence of neurotransmitters such as dopamine, serotonin, and norepinephrine in modulating cognitive schemas and their associated emotional valence. Dysregulation of these neurotransmitter systems has been implicated in the perturbation of schema processing, contributing to the persistence of negative or distorted schemas characteristic of depressive states.

The burgeoning field of epigenetics has unveiled the molecular mechanisms through which environmental factors can leave enduring marks on gene expression, potentially influencing the predisposition to certain schema patterns. This intersection of genetics, neurobiology, and environmental influences offers a comprehensive framework for understanding the multifaceted origins of schemas, emphasizing the need for an integrative approach that encompasses biological, psychological, and environmental factors.

## Mechanisms of Schema Activation in Depressive States

1. Neurobiological Correlates of Schema Activation:

Research into the neurobiological correlates of schema activation in depressive states has revealed intriguing connections between brain function and psychological processes. Neuroimaging studies have provided valuable insights into the neural underpinnings of how maladaptive schemas are triggered and perpetuated in individuals experiencing depression. One key focus of investigation has been the involvement of the limbic system, particularly the amygdala, in the activation of negative schemas. The amygdala's role in processing emotions and modulating responses to stress and threat stimuli implicates it as a pivotal structure in the schema activation process. Additionally, aberrant functioning of the prefrontal cortex, which governs cognitive control and emotion regulation, has been linked to heightened reactivity to schema-related triggers in individuals with depression. This dysfunctional interplay between the amygdala and the prefrontal cortex sheds light on the neurobiological basis of how certain environmental or internal cues elicit maladaptive schema activation in depressive states. Furthermore, studies have identified alterations in dopaminergic and serotonergic neurotransmission pathways that influence the salience and emotional significance attributed to schema-related stimuli. These neurochemical mechanisms contribute to the amplification of schema activation processes and underscore the interplay between neurobiology and psychological distress. Parallel investigations into the impact of chronic stress on neuroplasticity have unveiled how prolonged exposure to stressors can engender structural and functional changes within brain regions associated with emotional processing and memory consolidation, consequently heightening susceptibility to recurrent schema activation in depression. Understanding the neurobiological underpinnings of schema activation not only enriches our comprehension of the etiology of depressive disorders but also holds profound implications for the development of targeted interventions. By elucidating the neural circuitry involved in schema activation, novel therapeutic strategies can be devised to modulate these pathways and mitigate the intensity and frequency of maladaptive schema retrieval, offering renewed hope for individuals grappling with the debilitating effects of depression.

2. Cognitive Triggers and Automatic Thought Patterns:

Cognitive triggers and automatic thought patterns play a pivotal role in the activation of maladaptive schemas associated with depressive states. These triggers can stem from various cognitive processes, including but not limited to, selective attention, memory biases, and interpretive styles. When individuals with depression encounter situations that resonate with their deeply ingrained negative schemas, cognitive triggers activate automatic thought patterns that perpetuate and reinforce these maladaptive beliefs. Thus, it becomes essential to delve into the interplay between cognition and emotional processing within the context of schema activation.

Selective attention, a cognitive trigger, influences how individuals focus on information congruent with their pre-existing schemas while disregarding or distorting conflicting evidence. This tunnel vision further strengthens the negative cognitive bias inherent in their schemas, fostering a cyclical pattern of reinforcing negative thoughts. Memory biases, on the other hand, contribute to the skewed recollection and interpretation of past events, aligning them with the individual's maladaptive schemas, thus maintaining their negative worldview. Moreover, interpretive styles, such as overgeneralization, catastrophizing, and personalization, serve as automatic thought patterns that prompt distorted reasoning and lead to heightened emotional distress. It is through these cognitive triggers and automatic thought patterns that maladaptive schemas are vigorously activated in depressive states.

Recognizing and understanding these cognitive triggers and automatic thought patterns holds significant implications for therapeutic interventions. By targeting these mechanisms, cognitive-behavioral approaches can help individuals identify, challenge, and modify their automatic thought patterns, thereby disrupting the cycle of schema activation and reducing the intensity of depressive symptoms. Through targeted cognitive restructuring and cognitive defusion techniques, individuals can learn to reevaluate their cognitive triggers and manage them more adaptively, ultimately mitigating the impact of maladaptive schemas.

3. Role of Emotional Responses in Schema Activation:

Emotions play a crucial role in the activation of maladaptive schemas within individuals experiencing depressive states. These emotional responses often serve as potent triggers, precipitating a cascade of cognitive and behavioral patterns that are intimately linked with the individual's deeply ingrained schemas. Understanding the interplay between emotions and schema activation is pivotal in comprehending the vulnerabilities associated with depression. When an individual encounters emotionally charged situations or stimuli, their affective responses can act as catalysts for schema activation. For instance, feelings of inadequacy or worthlessness may be triggered by seemingly innocuous events, leading to a rapid reinforcement of negative self-schemas. Moreover, intense emotional states, such as sadness, despair, or hopelessness, can heighten the accessibility and salience of maladaptive schemas, further perpetuating the cycle of depressive cognitions and behaviors. It is essential to recognize that emotional responses do not occur in isolation; rather, they are inextricably intertwined with an individual's cognitive processes. This symbiotic relationship between emotions and cognition underscores the profound impact of emotional responses in perpetuating schema activation. Furthermore, emotional responses can significantly influence an individual's attentional focus, memory retrieval, and interpretation of ongoing events, thereby exacerbating the influence of maladaptive schemas. The link between emotions and schema activation extends beyond intrapersonal dynamics and encompasses interpersonal interactions as well. Emotional responses elicited in social contexts can serve as potent triggers for schema activation, particularly in the presence of perceived criticism, rejection, or invalidation. These interpersonal emotional experiences can reinforce negative relational schemas and augment the individual's vulnerability to depressive episodes. Additionally, the pervasive nature of emotional responses across various life domains implicates their substantial impact on schema activation. Whether in familial, occupational, or social settings, emotional experiences intrinsically shape the cognitive-affective patterns that underpin schema activation in depressive states. Recognizing the pivotal role of emotional responses in schema activation underscores the imperative for comprehensive therapeutic interventions that address both cognitive restructuring and emotional regulation strategies to effectively mitigate the impact of maladaptive schemas in depression.

4. Environmental and Situational Contributors:

The physical and social environments that individuals inhabit can significantly impact their emotional well-being and cognitive functioning, thus influencing the activation and reinforcement of negative schemas. One influential aspect of environmental contributors is the daily life stressors that individuals encounter. Stressful events, such as academic or occupational challenges, financial difficulties, family conflicts, or health-related concerns, can serve as potent triggers for activating maladaptive schemas. These stressors elicit negative emotions and cognitions, which reinforce pre-existing negative self-views and beliefs, ultimately perpetuating the individual's depressive state. Understanding the role of these stressors in schema activation is crucial for developing targeted interventions aimed at mitigating their impact on mental well-being.

The quality of interpersonal relationships within one's environment profoundly influences the activation of maladaptive schemas. Negative interactions with family members, friends, or colleagues can validate individuals' negative self-perceptions and contribute to a cycle of negative reinforcement. For instance, repeated experiences of criticism, rejection, or invalidation from significant others can foster an enduring sense of worthlessness or unlovability, reinforcing corresponding maladaptive schemas. Conversely, positive and supportive social interactions can serve as protective factors against the activation of maladaptive schemas, promoting resilience and psychological well-being.

In addition to social dynamics, the physical surroundings in which individuals live and work can also impact schema activation. Living in disordered or unsafe environments, experiencing chronic noise or crowding, or enduring long periods of solitude can create additional emotional and cognitive burdens, further fueling the activation of maladaptive schemas. Likewise, exposure to traumatic events or adversities, such as natural disasters or community violence, can significantly heighten vulnerability to depressive symptoms by amplifying the activation of maladaptive schemas.

5. Interpersonal Dynamics Influencing Schema Activation:

The interactions and relationships that an individual engages in can significantly impact their cognitive processes and emotional well-being, contributing to the reinforcement or disruption of these negative schemas. One significant aspect of interpersonal dynamics is the concept of attachment styles. Research has found that insecure attachment styles, characterized by patterns of avoidance or anxiety, are associated with the development of maladaptive schemas related to abandonment, rejection, and inadequacy. Moreover, individuals with such attachment styles may seek out relationships that inadvertently reinforce these schemas, perpetuating a cycle of negative interaction patterns and emotional distress.

Communication patterns within interpersonal relationships can serve as triggers for schema activation. Criticism, invalidation, or conflict-laden exchanges can fuel cognitive distortions and elicit strong emotional responses, intensifying the influence of maladaptive schemas. Inadequate support and empathy from significant others can also contribute to the maintenance of negative self-perceptions and beliefs, amplifying the impact of these schemas on the individual's psychological well-being.

The power dynamics within relationships also hold significance in schema activation. Individuals who experience a sense of powerlessness or subjugation in their interactions with others may develop schemas centered on worthlessness, unimportance, or a lack of control. These relational dynamics can perpetuate feelings of helplessness and hopelessness, reinforcing the negative cognitive frameworks and emotional responses associated with depression. Furthermore, the presence of coercive or abusive behaviors in relationships can significantly exacerbate the activation and reinforcement of maladaptive schemas, further entrenching the individual in a cycle of psychological distress.

In addition to these individual dynamics, family systems and social networks can significantly influence schema activation. Environments characterized by dysfunction, conflict, or neglect can cultivate and reinforce maladaptive cognitive schemas, creating a pervasive context for the persistence of depressive symptoms. Conversely, supportive, validating, and secure social environments can serve as protective factors, mitigating the impact of maladaptive schemas and fostering adaptive coping strategies.

6. Cycle of Reactivation - Depressive Episodes:

Depressive episodes often serve as catalysts for the reactivation of deeply ingrained maladaptive schemas, creating a feedback loop that sustains the individual's experience of depression. This cyclical pattern can manifest in various ways, contributing to the persistence and exacerbation of depressive symptoms over time. The triggering of maladaptive schemas during depressive episodes often leads to heightened emotional distress, distorted thinking patterns, and negative behavioral responses, further reinforcing the individual's negative self-concept and world view.

As the individual continues to experience these reinforced schemas during each depressive episode, the cycle of reactivation becomes increasingly entrenched, making it more difficult for the individual to disrupt the pattern and achieve lasting relief from their symptoms. Moreover, the cycle of reactivation can lead to a gradual intensification of the individual's depressive episodes, as the prolonged reinforcement of maladaptive schemas deepens their influence on the individual's cognitive and emotional processing. This deepening impact can significantly impede the individual's ability to engage in adaptive coping strategies, maintain healthy interpersonal relationships, and cope with life stressors effectively. Recognizing the interplay between depressive episodes and the reactivation of maladaptive schemas is essential for clinicians and researchers seeking to develop targeted interventions that interrupt this cycle and promote lasting recovery. By addressing the cycle of reactivation, clinicians can work toward empowering individuals to recognize, challenge, and ultimately transform their maladaptive schemas, reducing the frequency and severity of depressive episodes. Additionally, fostering resilience and enhancing adaptive coping mechanisms can help individuals manage future challenges without succumbing to the detrimental effects of recurrent schema reactivation.

7. Longitudinal Impact on the Individual:

The concept of schemas and their activation in depressive states raises important considerations about the longitudinal impact on individuals. Longitudinal studies provide valuable insights into how activated schemas perpetuate and influence an individual's psychological well-being over extended periods. These studies delve into the lasting effects of schema activation on cognitive processes, emotional responses, and behavioral patterns. By observing individuals over time, researchers can better understand the sustained influence of activated schemas on the development and maintenance of depressive episodes. Longitudinal investigations also shed light on the potential for recurrent or chronic schemas to impact an individual's adaptive functioning and overall quality of life. Additionally, longitudinal assessments offer a comprehensive view of how schema activation may contribute to the progression or recurrence of depressive symptoms, providing crucial information for personalized treatment planning and intervention strategies. Moreover, examining the longitudinal impact of schema activation allows for the identification of protective factors and resilience mechanisms that may mitigate the detrimental consequences of maladaptive schemas. This understanding is vital for clinicians and practitioners seeking to tailor therapeutic approaches to address the enduring effects of schema activation on individual mental health. Furthermore, longitudinal research contributes to the elucidation of potential trajectories of schema activation across various life stages and transitional periods, offering critical insights into the dynamic nature of schemas and their implications for long-term psychological well-being. Understanding the longitudinal impact of schema activation on the individual is pivotal for advancing clinical practices and informing preventive measures that promote mental health resilience. It provides a foundation for developing targeted interventions that aim to disrupt the cycle of schema reactivation and foster enduring positive changes in individuals' cognitive-affective processes.

## Types of Maladaptive Schemas Linked to Depression

1. Specific Vulnerability Domains:

Specific vulnerability domains encapsulate clusters of core beliefs and assumptions through which individuals perceive themselves, others, and the world around them. One prominent vulnerability domain pertains to the perception of oneself as inherently flawed or defective. This encompasses deeply ingrained beliefs that one is fundamentally unworthy, inadequate, or unlovable, often manifesting as overwhelming feelings of shame and self-criticism. Individuals harboring such beliefs may engage in self-sabotaging behaviors, struggle with establishing fulfilling relationships, and experience persistent distress regarding their perceived shortcomings.

Another critical vulnerability domain revolves around the fear of rejection, abandonment, or betrayal. Rooted in past relational experiences, individuals carrying these schemas may approach interpersonal interactions with trepidation and an underlying sense of impending loss. This pervasive apprehension can give rise to patterns of emotional withdrawal, dependence, or an inability to trust, perpetuating a cycle of loneliness and social challenges.

The domain of autonomy and performance issues encompasses beliefs surrounding one's competence, efficacy, and capacity for independent functioning. Those impacted by this vulnerability domain often grapple with feelings of helplessness, incapacity, and an overarching sense of being inept at managing life's demands. Consequently, they may exhibit avoidant tendencies, struggle with decision-making processes, and harbor persistent doubts about their ability to manage challenges effectively.

Within the context of specific vulnerability domains, it is crucial to address the pervasive themes of entitlement and unmet needs. Individuals shaped by entitlement schemas may experience profound dissatisfaction and frustration when their expectations are not met, leading to interpersonal conflicts and a perpetual sense of disillusionment. Understanding the underpinnings of such entitlement perceptions enables clinicians to discern the connection between unmet needs and the resultant emotional distress, thereby informing targeted interventions to foster adaptive coping strategies and realistic expectations.

At the heart of understanding specific vulnerability domains lies the recognition of how these deeply entrenched beliefs and cognitive patterns contribute to the maintenance of depressive states. Recognizing the multifaceted nature of these vulnerabilities allows for the tailored application of therapeutic strategies aimed at restructuring maladaptive schemas, fostering resilience, and engendering positive self-concept and relational dynamics.

2. Emotional Deprivation Schema:

The emotional deprivation schema, a significant maladaptive schema linked to depression, encompasses an individual's core belief of not receiving adequate emotional support, nurturing, or empathy from others. This pervasive belief often stems from early experiences of neglect, emotional unavailability, or invalidation, and can significantly influence an individual's cognitive and emotional processing. Understanding the emotional deprivation schema necessitates delving into its manifestation across various aspects of an individual's life, including interpersonal relationships, self-perception, and coping mechanisms.

One characteristic manifestation of the emotional deprivation schema is the tendency to seek excessive validation and approval from external sources, as individuals with this schema may perceive themselves as inherently unworthy or undeserving of genuine care and understanding. Consequently, they may exhibit behaviors aimed at eliciting the desired emotional support, inadvertently perpetuating a cycle of unmet needs and reinforcing their core belief of emotional deprivation. Additionally, individuals harboring this schema may struggle with establishing and maintaining authentic connections, often feeling unfulfilled or dissatisfied in their relationships due to an ongoing perceived deficit of emotional sustenance.

The emotional deprivation schema contributes to a profound sense of inner emptiness and chronic longing for emotional fulfillment. This pervasive emotional void may lead individuals to engage in compensatory behaviors, such as overeating, substance abuse, or excessive work, in an attempt to alleviate their emotional distress. Despite these efforts, the deep-seated belief of inherent emotional scarcity persists, perpetuating a state of chronic emotional distress and cognitive rumination.

From a cognitive standpoint, individuals influenced by the emotional deprivation schema frequently adopt a filter that amplifies instances of perceived emotional neglect or rejection while discounting expressions of genuine care and support, reinforcing their negative core belief. This cognitive bias heightens susceptibility to depressive symptomatology, as it intensifies feelings of isolation and unworthiness, diminishing one's resilience in coping with adversities.

The emotional deprivation schema profoundly influences an individual's self-perception and identity formation. The pervasive belief of being emotionally deprived may lead to internalized feelings of inadequacy, unworthiness, and defective self-worth. As a result, individuals may develop stringent self-imposed standards and engage in relentless self-criticism, perpetuating a cycle of diminished self-value and exacerbating depressive symptoms.

Efficiently addressing the emotional deprivation schema within the therapeutic context involves an integrated approach that encompasses cognitive restructuring, emotion-focused interventions, and relational techniques. By fostering an environment that validates the individual's emotional experiences and promotes self-compassion, therapists can aid in challenging and transforming the deeply ingrained perceptions of emotional scarcity, thereby fostering healthier and more adaptive modes of relating to oneself and others.

3. Abandonment and Instability Patterns:

Abandonment and instability are central themes within maladaptive schemas linked to depression, encompassing detrimental perceptions of enduring loss and unpredictability. These schemas often develop from real or perceived experiences of neglect, rejection, or inconsistent caregiving during formative years, leading to an ingrained belief in the inevitability of desertion and upheaval in relationships and life circumstances. Such deep-seated belief systems can significantly impact an individual's sense of self-worth, trust in others, and ability to cultivate secure and stable connections.

Individuals harboring abandonment and instability schemas might display tendencies towards clinginess or possessiveness in relationships as a means to mitigate their underlying fear of being abandoned. Conversely, they might also exhibit patterns of emotional detachment or avoidance as a protective response to anticipated loss. These coping mechanisms, while initially adaptive, can perpetuate a cycle of relational distress and reinforce the pervasive nature of the schema.

The manifestation of abandonment and instability schemas extends beyond interpersonal dynamics to engender a general sense of uncertainty and apprehension about future prospects. Individuals influenced by these schemas may struggle to maintain stability in various domains of their lives, including career aspirations, personal goals, and emotional well-being. This perpetual state of instability can exacerbate feelings of helplessness and hopelessness, subsequently predisposing individuals to the onset or perpetuation of depressive symptoms.

Recognizing and addressing these deeply entrenched abandonment and instability patterns is pivotal in therapeutic interventions aimed at alleviating depressive symptoms. Through targeted cognitive restructuring and experiential techniques, individuals can gradually reframe their interpretations of relational dynamics and cultivate a more nuanced understanding of stability and attachment. Integrating these strategies with emotion-focused therapies enables individuals to process and manage their emotional responses towards fostering healthier relational patterns and bolstering resilience against the insidious influence of abandonment and instability schemas.

4. Defectiveness and Shame Schema Dynamics:

Defectiveness and shame schema dynamics are intrinsically linked to the core beliefs that individuals hold about their fundamental worth. These schemas often stem from early experiences of rejection, criticism, or emotional neglect, leading individuals to develop pervasive feelings of inadequacy and unworthiness. At the heart of these maladaptive schemas is a profound sense of flaw or defect that permeates various aspects of one's self-concept. Individuals with such schemas frequently harbor persistent feelings of not measuring up, being inherently flawed, or feeling unlovable. These sentiments can significantly impact their interpersonal relationships, self-esteem, and overall psychological well-being. Moreover, the shame associated with these perceptions tends to reinforce a cycle of self-criticism and withdrawal, perpetuating the negative impact of the schema. It is imperative to recognize that these maladaptive schemas operate at both conscious and unconscious levels, exerting a potent influence on an individual's emotional responses, cognitive processing, and behavioral patterns. Seemingly unrelated events or interactions can trigger deep-seated shame reactions, eliciting defensive behaviors or avoidance strategies as a means of self-preservation. Addressing defectiveness and shame schema dynamics in the context of depression requires a multifaceted approach encompassing cognitive restructuring, emotion regulation, and compassionate self-acceptance. By fostering a therapeutic environment that encourages vulnerability, validation, and reframing of negative self-perceptions, individuals can begin to challenge and restructure these entrenched maladaptive schemas. Comprehensive interventions that integrate experiential techniques, exploration of early experiences, and nurturing of self-compassion can facilitate the gradual unraveling of these deeply ingrained belief systems. Clinicians and mental health professionals play a pivotal role in supporting individuals in reframing their internal narratives, cultivating self-empowerment, and fostering a sense of belonging and acceptance.

5. Dependence and Incompetence Perceptions:

Within the context of cognitive models, dependence and incompetence perceptions contribute significantly to an individual's overall sense of self-worth and personal efficacy. Dependence schema encompasses a belief that one is incapable of functioning autonomously or meeting basic needs without external support or validation. This often contributes to feelings of helplessness and inadequacy, perpetuating a cycle of self-doubt and reliance on others for emotional well-being. Similarly, incompetence schema revolves around the pervasive perception of being fundamentally inadequate or inept in various domains of life, such as work, relationships, and decision-making. These beliefs can evoke profound feelings of failure and unworthiness, amplifying the experience of depression and diminishing the individual's motivation to pursue meaningful goals. It is essential to recognize that these maladaptive schemas are not just isolated thoughts or beliefs; they deeply shape an individual's emotional responses, behavior patterns, and interpersonal dynamics. Moreover, the interplay between dependence and incompetence perceptions often exacerbates the individual's vulnerability to depressive symptoms. For instance, a person grappling with entrenched feelings of incompetence may seek excessive reassurance from others, reinforcing their dependence schema and further deepening their sense of inadequacy. Understanding the nuanced manifestations and origins of these schemas is crucial for clinicians and researchers aiming to address the multifaceted nature of depression. Therapeutic strategies tailored to target dependence and incompetence perceptions may involve cognitive restructuring, behavioral activation, and fostering adaptive coping mechanisms. By challenging distorted beliefs and cultivating self-reliance, individuals can gradually mitigate the impact of these maladaptive schemas, empowering them to manage life's challenges with increased resilience and agency.

6. Significance of Entitlement Perceptions:

Entitlement perceptions, within the framework of maladaptive schemas linked to depression, revolve around the belief that one is inherently deserving of special treatment, superior recognition, or unearned privileges without commensurate effort or contribution. Such distortions in thinking often stem from early experiences of indulgence, unrealistic praise, or overprotection, fostering an inflated sense of entitlement. This distorted cognitive lens fosters a pervasive sense of unfairness when reality fails to meet exaggerated expectations, fueling feelings of dissatisfaction, resentment, and disillusionment when faced with ordinary challenges or setbacks. Individuals harboring entitlement perceptions may struggle to accept personal responsibility, resulting in strained interpersonal relationships and hindered self-development. Moreover, these maladaptive beliefs can exacerbate the severity and persistence of depressive symptoms, as individuals grapple with unmet expectations and perpetuated disillusionment. Understanding the significance of entitlement perceptions necessitates a multi-dimensional approach, encompassing cognitive restructuring, behavioral interventions, and nuanced exploration of upbringing and societal influences. Therapeutic strategies aimed at addressing entitlement perceptions involve cultivating accountability, fostering empathy towards others, and promoting a more realistic appraisal of personal rights and privileges. Clinicians must manage the delicate balance between acknowledging an individual's distress while challenging entitled cognitions to promote adaptive coping and internal locus of control.

### Interplay Between Schemas and Cognitive Distortions

1. Schemas vs. Cognitive Distortions – Identification of the Overlap:

As we know, schemas and cognitive distortions are integral components of the cognitive model, playing crucial roles in a person's emotional experiences and behaviors. While schemas represent enduring core beliefs about oneself and the world, cognitive distortions are specific thinking errors that contribute to negative interpretations of events.

To comprehend the convergence of schemas and cognitive distortions, it is essential to acknowledge their shared influence on information processing. Schemas form a cognitive framework through which individuals interpret and organize incoming information, shaping their perceptions and judgments. Simultaneously, cognitive distortions skew an individual's thought patterns, leading to biased processing of information that aligns with their existing schemas. The amalgamation of these processes can significantly impact an individual's emotional responses and behavioral reactions in various situations.

Exploring the overlap between schemas and cognitive distortions entails examining the reciprocal relationship between the two constructs. As individuals' core beliefs (schemas) predispose them to interpret situations in specific ways, cognitive distortions reinforce and perpetuate these maladaptive interpretations, thereby strengthening the influence of schemas. Conversely, the presence of cognitive distortions can intensify the activation of pre-existing maladaptive schemas, creating a feedback loop that sustains negative cognitive-emotional patterns.

In clinical settings, delineating the distinction between schemas and cognitive distortions is vital for formulating targeted interventions. Therapists need to discern whether a client's presenting issues stem from rigid schema-related beliefs or from cognitive distortions that distort their perception of reality. By identifying the primary contributing factor, therapists can tailor therapeutic strategies to dispute cognitive distortions or modify maladaptive schemas, thereby promoting more adaptive cognitive processes and emotional well-being.

Understanding the interplay between schemas and cognitive distortions can enrich therapeutic approaches such as cognitive restructuring and schema-focused interventions. Integrating strategies that specifically address and disentangle the interconnectedness of these factors enables a comprehensive and nuanced treatment approach. By dismantling the reinforcing cycle between maladaptive schemas and cognitive distortions, individuals can cultivate more flexible and balanced cognitive appraisals, reducing the emotional toll of underlying mental health difficulties.

2. Mechanisms of Interaction:

In exploring the interplay between schemas and cognitive distortions, it is essential to delve into the mechanisms that underpin their interaction. Schemas, deeply ingrained cognitive structures shaped by early experiences, significantly impact an individual's perception and interpretation of incoming information. Simultaneously, cognitive distortions, characterized by biased or skewed thought patterns, can further exacerbate the activation and perpetuation of maladaptive schemas.

Central to the understanding of the interactive mechanisms are the cognitive processes involved in filtering, interpreting, and processing information. The cognitive biases inherent in individuals with maladaptive schemas often lead to the selective encoding, retention, and recall of information that reinforces pre-existing negative beliefs, thereby perpetuating a cycle of distorted thinking and emotional distress. Moreover, the reciprocal reinforcement between maladaptive schemas and cognitive distortions can create a self-perpetuating system wherein the individual's experiences continue to align with and reinforce their preconceived negative worldview.

The cognitive-affective processes play a pivotal role in operationalizing the interaction between schemas and cognitive distortions. Emotional factors heavily influence the interpretation and evaluation of one's experiences, subsequently influencing the activation and maintenance of maladaptive schemas. Understanding how emotional states can shape cognitive processes and vice versa provides crucial insights into the bidirectional nature of the interplay.

Importantly, environmental and situational triggers also contribute to the activation and modulation of these interactive mechanisms. Stressful events, interpersonal dynamics, and environmental cues can elicit and perpetuate maladaptive schema activation, further intertwining with cognitive distortions to shape an individual's perception and behavioral responses. Recognizing the contextual influences on the interplay between schemas and cognitive distortions is indispensable for comprehensively understanding the complexities of this dynamic relationship.

3. Implicative Outcomes in Psychopathology:

The interplay between schemas and cognitive distortions unfolds a complex trajectory within psychopathological manifestations. At the core of implicative outcomes lies the web of how deeply ingrained schemas fuel and perpetuate cognitive distortions, leading to a cascade of adverse effects on an individual's mental health. These implicative outcomes can manifest in a myriad of ways, including but not limited to exacerbating symptoms, prolonging episodes, or impeding recovery in individuals with depressive disorders, anxiety disorders, post-traumatic stress disorder (PTSD), and other related conditions. By elucidating the pathways through which maladaptive schemas and cognitive distortions contribute to the onset and maintenance of such psychopathologies, we can discern the complexities underlying these mental health challenges.

Implicative outcomes extend beyond symptomatology to affect broader areas of an individual's life, encompassing interpersonal relationships, occupational functioning, and overall quality of life. The pervasive nature of these implicative outcomes underscores the imperative need to address the interplay between schemas and cognitive distortions in clinical practice and therapeutic interventions. Recognizing the far-reaching implications of these maladaptive cognitive processes is fundamental in designing comprehensive treatment approaches that not only target symptom reduction but also mitigate the broader impact on an individual's well-being.

Exploring the implicative outcomes in psychopathology sheds light on the potential prognostic relevance of identifying and addressing maladaptive schemas and cognitive distortions. Understanding how these implicative outcomes influence the course and prognosis of various psychological disorders can inform tailored interventions aimed at disrupting the deleterious cycle of maladaptive cognitive patterns. This proactive approach holds promise in enhancing treatment efficacy and promoting sustained mental wellness.

4. Analytical Models for Assessing Synergy:

The interplay between schemas and cognitive distortions presents a complex dynamic that requires thorough analysis to understand its synergistic impact on psychopathology. To achieve this, analytical models offer a structured approach to dissect the relationship between these two core components of psychological functioning. These models aim to provide a comprehensive framework for evaluating the combined influence of schemas and cognitive distortions on an individual's cognitive, emotional, and behavioral patterns.

One prominent analytical model is the Schema-Cognitive Distortion Interaction Model (SCDIM), which delves into the reciprocal interactions between maladaptive schemas and cognitive distortions. SCDIM posits that certain cognitive distortions can serve as triggers, activating specific maladaptive schemas, thus exacerbating cognitive vulnerabilities and perpetuating negative affective states. By delineating these interactions, SCDIM facilitates a deeper understanding of how particular cognitive distortions may reinforce pre-existing maladaptive schemas, leading to a perpetuation of dysfunctional beliefs and behaviors.

Another instrumental model is the Multidimensional Schema Therapy Model (MSTM), which integrates cognitive distortions within the broader context of schema therapy. MSTM adopts a multidimensional perspective, considering various factors such as early life experiences, coping styles, and interpersonal dynamics, to elucidate how cognitive distortions interact with maladaptive schemas across different domains of an individual's life. This integrative approach allows for a nuanced evaluation of the interdependent nature of schemas and cognitive distortions, shedding light on their joint impact on emotional regulation and interpersonal functioning.

On the other hand, the Cognitive Schema-Distortion Integration Framework (CSDIF) offers a heuristic model for synthesizing cognitive distortions within the framework of core maladaptive schemas. CSDIF advocates for the identification of specific cognitive distortions that frequently co-occur with distinct maladaptive schemas, thereby illuminating the correspondence between cognitive distortions and underlying core beliefs. This integrated approach underscores the need to address cognitive distortions in tandem with targeting maladaptive schemas, recognizing the complementary roles they play in shaping an individual's cognitive-emotional landscape.

5. Therapeutic Interventions:

The complex interplay between schemas and cognitive distortions presents a profound challenge in the sphere of therapeutic interventions. Addressing this duality requires a multifaceted approach that integrates targeted strategies to modify maladaptive schemas while simultaneously addressing underlying cognitive distortions.

Cognitive restructuring, a cornerstone of cognitive behavioral therapy, serves as a primary modality for addressing the cognitive distortions intertwined with maladaptive schemas. By systematically identifying and challenging irrational beliefs, individuals can restructure their cognitive frameworks, thereby disrupting the cycle of reinforcing negative schemas. Additionally, mindfulness-based interventions have shown promise in targeting both the rigid nature of maladaptive schemas and the automatic thoughts associated with cognitive distortions. Through cultivating non-judgmental awareness, individuals gain the capacity to observe their thoughts and emotions without becoming enmeshed in cognitive distortions, thus fostering a more flexible cognitive response.

Schema-focused therapy, an integrative approach specifically designed to target maladaptive schemas, offers a framework for directly addressing deep-rooted, negative core beliefs. By combining cognitive, behavioral, and experiential techniques, this approach facilitates the modification of maladaptive schemas, ultimately leading to more adaptive responses in various life situations. Schema-focused therapy holds particular relevance in addressing the relationship between schemas and cognitive distortions due to its emphasis on targeting the core themes that underpin these cognitive processes.

In addition to these primary interventions, the incorporation of emotion-focused techniques plays a crucial role in addressing the affective components associated with maladaptive schemas and cognitive distortions. Emotion-focused interventions aim to facilitate emotional processing, fostering a deeper understanding and acceptance of underlying emotions. By creating new emotional experiences within the therapeutic context, individuals can challenge and modify the emotional responses linked to both maladaptive schemas and cognitive distortions.

It is essential for clinicians to consider the complete integration of these therapeutic interventions when addressing the duality of schemas and cognitive distortions. By combining cognitive restructuring, mindfulness-based techniques, schema-focused therapy, and emotion-focused interventions, clinicians can effectively target the interconnected cognitive and affective factors contributing to psychological distress, ultimately fostering profound change in individuals' cognitive-emotional systems.

**The Impact of Schemas in Clinical Settings**

1. Quantitative Methods - Surveys and Questionnaires:

The utilization of quantitative methods, such as surveys and questionnaires, in assessing the impact of schemas in clinical settings represents a pivotal aspect of contemporary research and practice. Through structured data collection techniques, researchers and mental health professionals can gain invaluable insights into the prevalence, nature, and influence of maladaptive schemas on individuals experiencing depression. Surveys and questionnaires provide a systematic means of gathering information related to an individual's cognitive structures, beliefs, and cognitive patterns, allowing for the formulation of empirical assessments and comparisons across diverse populations.

When designing surveys and questionnaires to measure the impact of schemas, it is crucial to ensure that the instruments are grounded in theoretical frameworks and exhibit robust psychometric properties. By employing established scales and validated measures, professionals can effectively capture the nuances of maladaptive schemas while maintaining reliability and validity in their findings. Furthermore, the use of standardized instruments facilitates the aggregation of data, enabling researchers to draw meaningful conclusions regarding the relationship between specific schema profiles and depressive symptomatology.

Quantitative methods also afford the opportunity to quantify the severity and pervasiveness of maladaptive schemas, shedding light on the differential impact of various cognitive distortions on an individual's emotional wellbeing. Through the administration of structured assessments, clinicians can systematically evaluate the presence of core beliefs, early maladaptive schemas, and automatic thoughts, thereby informing targeted interventions and treatment planning tailored to address the specific cognitive vulnerabilities identified. Additionally, the systematic nature of surveys and questionnaires enables the identification of potential comorbidities and the exploration of how maladaptive schemas intersect with other psychological disorders, contributing to a comprehensive understanding of a client's mental health status.

It is important to acknowledge the limitations of quantitative methods, including the potential for response bias, social desirability effects, and oversimplification of complex cognitive processes. Therefore, triangulating quantitative findings with qualitative data and clinical observations becomes imperative for gaining a holistic understanding of an individual's schema-related experiences. By synthesizing quantitative and qualitative insights, professionals can enrich their conceptualization of the multifaceted nature of maladaptive schemas, paving the way for more nuanced and individualized intervention strategies.

As research continues to advance, the refinement of quantitative methodologies in measuring the impact of schemas will undoubtedly contribute to the ongoing evolution of evidence-based practices in the field of psychology and mental health. The judicious integration of surveys and questionnaires within clinical assessments bolsters our capacity to discern the interplay between schemas and depression, ultimately fostering more targeted and effective therapeutic interventions.

2. Qualitative Approaches - Interviews and Case Studies:

Qualitative approaches to measuring the impact of schemas in clinical settings provide valuable insights into the nature of individuals' cognitive and emotional processes. Interviews and case studies allow researchers and clinicians to delve deeply into the lived experiences of individuals, capturing nuances that quantitative methods may overlook. Conducting in-depth interviews with individuals affected by depression can unveil the underlying schemas that shape their perceptions, beliefs, and behaviors. These interviews often involve open-ended questions that encourage participants to reflect on their thought patterns and emotional responses in various life situations. The richness of qualitative data obtained through these interviews enables a comprehensive understanding of how maladaptive schemas manifest and influence the experience of depression. Furthermore, case studies offer a detailed exploration of individual cases, providing a thorough examination of the interplay between specific schemas and depressive symptoms. By immersing in the narratives of individual cases, clinicians can gain profound insights into the unique ways in which schemas contribute to the onset and maintenance of depression. Detailed exploration of the personal history, cognitive patterns, and emotional triggers within the context of case studies enhances our comprehension of the complex relationships between schemas and psychological well-being. Moreover, qualitative approaches foster an empathetic understanding of the human experience of depression, contributing to a more holistic and patient-centered approach to assessment and treatment. Through the systematic analysis of qualitative data, themes and patterns related to schemas in depression can be identified, leading to the development of more targeted interventions. Additionally, the integration of qualitative findings with quantitative measures strengthens the validity and reliability of schema assessments in clinical practice. While qualitative approaches offer in-depth exploration, they also present certain challenges, such as the potential for bias in interpretation and the time-consuming nature of data analysis. However, when used in conjunction with quantitative methods, the insights gained from qualitative approaches enrich the comprehensive evaluation of schemas in clinical settings, informing personalized and effective interventions for individuals experiencing depression.

3. Standardized Tools for Measuring Schemas:

Standardized tools for measuring schemas provide valuable insights into an individual's cognitive structures and beliefs that may contribute to depressive symptoms. These tools offer a systematic and reliable means of assessing maladaptive schemas across diverse populations, enabling clinicians and researchers to gain a comprehensive understanding of their influence. One prominent standardized tool is the Young Schema Questionnaire (YSQ), developed by Dr. Jeffrey Young. This questionnaire consists of 205 items designed to assess 18 early maladaptive schemas commonly associated with depression and other psychological disorders. The YSQ has demonstrated strong psychometric properties and has been widely used in both clinical and research settings to identify and measure maladaptive schemas. Another widely utilized tool is the Schema Mode Inventory (SMI), which evaluates different schema modes or coping styles adopted by individuals in response to emotional triggers. This instrument provides a nuanced assessment of how individuals experience and respond to their maladaptive schemas, offering valuable insight for tailored therapeutic interventions. Moreover, the Schema Therapy Rating Scale (STRS) is employed to assess therapist competencies in delivering schema therapy and adherence to its principles. By evaluating therapeutic processes, the STRS contributes to the refinement and improvement of schema-focused interventions, ultimately enhancing treatment outcomes. Additionally, the Schema Questionnaire for Children (SQ-C) has been developed to assess maladaptive schemas in younger populations, recognizing the importance of early intervention and prevention strategies. The utilization of standardized tools for measuring schemas in diverse clinical settings has facilitated the identification of specific cognitive patterns associated with depression across different demographic groups, allowing for targeted interventions and personalized treatment approaches. However, it is essential to recognize the limitations of these tools, including potential cultural biases and the subjective nature of self-report measures. Ongoing research and development focused on enhancing the cultural sensitivity and validity of these tools are vital to ensure their applicability across diverse populations. As the field continues to evolve, the integration of advanced technologies and innovative assessment methods holds promise for further refining the measurement of schemas and advancing our understanding of their impact on depression.

4. Clinical Assessment Practices in Diverse Populations:

When working with diverse populations, clinicians are tasked with addressing cultural, linguistic, and contextual factors that can significantly influence the manifestation and expression of maladaptive schemas. To ensure accurate assessment, it is essential to employ culturally informed tools and techniques, as well as demonstrate cultural competence and sensitivity.

In clinical settings, conducting thorough assessments involves not only recognizing the presence of maladaptive schemas but also acknowledging their potential variations within different cultural contexts. This process requires an understanding of how cultural beliefs, values, and societal norms may shape individuals' experiences and interpretations of their schemas. Furthermore, language barriers and communication styles must be carefully considered when conducting assessments, as these factors can impact the validity and reliability of gathered data.

It is important for clinicians to recognize the nuances of assessing schemas in diverse populations and adopt an inclusive approach that respects individual differences. This entails incorporating culturally validated measures, engaging in active listening, and being attentive to nonverbal cues that may convey underlying schema-related distress. Additionally, collaborating with interpreters and culturally competent professionals can enhance the accuracy and depth of assessments, providing valuable insights into the unique ways schemas may manifest across diverse groups.

The assessment of schemas in diverse populations should extend beyond a mere identification of maladaptive patterns. Clinicians must strive to understand the sociocultural context in which schemas develop and persist, including the influence of systemic inequalities, discrimination, and acculturation experiences. By contextualizing schema assessment within broader social and environmental factors, clinicians can gain a more comprehensive understanding of the complexity of schemas within diverse populations and tailor interventions that effectively address these factors.

Culturally sensitive assessments not only contribute to a more accurate understanding of schemas but also lay the foundation for culturally responsive treatment planning. By recognizing the intersections of culture, identity, and psychological processes, clinicians can devise intervention strategies that resonate with diverse individuals, promoting inclusivity and efficacy in schema-focused therapeutic endeavors.

5. Challenges in Schema Measurement and Interpretation:

Schema measurement and interpretation in the context of clinical settings pose several challenges that require careful consideration. Firstly, discrepancies in the understanding and categorization of schemas across different theoretical frameworks can complicate the measurement process. This challenge is compounded by the need for standardized tools that can effectively capture the multifaceted nature of schemas and their impact on depression. Moreover, cultural and contextual variations in the expression and experience of schemas among diverse populations present a significant hurdle to accurate measurement and interpretation. Additionally, the dynamic and evolving nature of schemas over time necessitates longitudinal assessment methods, which can be resource-intensive and logistically complex. Furthermore, identifying and distinguishing between overlapping or interrelated schemas requires a sophisticated approach to interpretation, as these intricacies can have varying implications for treatment planning and intervention strategies. Another critical challenge involves the potential for clinician bias in interpreting schema assessment results, highlighting the importance of ongoing training and supervision to enhance objectivity and consistency in measurement. Ethical considerations related to the use of sensitive data obtained through schema assessments also demand careful attention and oversight, particularly in relation to privacy and confidentiality. Lastly, the integration of emerging technologies in schema measurement introduces both opportunities and challenges, as the field addresses ethical, reliability, and validity concerns associated with innovative assessment tools. Addressing these challenges requires collaboration among researchers, clinicians, and stakeholders to develop comprehensive and culturally sensitive approaches to schema measurement and interpretation in clinical practice. By acknowledging and actively engaging with these complexities, the field can advance its capacity to effectively assess and address maladaptive schemas in the context of depression.

6. Longitudinal Studies of Schema Impact on Depression:

Longitudinal studies are pivotal in understanding the long-term effects of schemas on depression. These rigorous research endeavors involve tracking individuals over extended periods, allowing for a comprehensive examination of how schemas contribute to the onset, maintenance, and recurrence of depressive episodes. By observing changes in maladaptive schema activation and the corresponding impact on depressive symptoms over time, researchers can gain valuable insights into the dynamic nature of these cognitive constructs. Longitudinal studies enable the identification of patterns and trends in schema evolvement, shedding light on the interplay between chronic schemas and the manifestation of depression across various life stages. Moreover, they provide a deeper understanding of the potential moderating and mediating factors influencing the trajectory of schema-driven depressive experiences. Furthermore, the longitudinal approach facilitates the assessment of individual differences in the susceptibility to schema-related distress, resilience factors, and the efficacy of interventions in altering maladaptive cognitive structures. These studies also offer crucial information on the stability of schemas, exploring whether certain schemas persist or transform over time and their differential impact on the chronicity and severity of depressive symptoms. Longitudinal research elucidates the bidirectional relationship between schemas and depression, unraveling how the persistence of maladaptive schemas may perpetuate a cycle of vulnerability to recurrent depressive episodes. Additionally, by examining the influence of environmental stressors, life events, and coping strategies on the interaction between schemas and depression, longitudinal studies provide a nuanced understanding of the contextual factors shaping the trajectory of psychological well-being. The findings from longitudinal studies have significant implications for clinical practice, informing the development of targeted interventions aimed at interrupting the negative schema-depression cycle. These insights guide the implementation of personalized treatment plans tailored to address the specific schema profiles and their impact on depressive symptomatology. Moreover, longitudinal research aids in forecasting the prognosis of individuals with distinct schema configurations, fostering the early identification of high-risk populations and the delivery of timely preventative measures. Through a multifaceted exploration of the long-term consequences of schemas on depression, longitudinal studies contribute invaluable data to the field of clinical psychology, guiding evidence-based strategies for optimizing mental health outcomes.

7. Integrating Multimodal Assessments in Practice:

In the sphere of clinical practice, the evaluation and assessment of maladaptive schemas have traditionally relied on a single modality, such as self-report measures or standardized questionnaires. However, the contemporary landscape of psychological assessment has seen a growing recognition of the need for integrated, multimodal approaches to capturing the nuances of schema impact.

Integrating multimodal assessments involves the convergence of various assessment tools and techniques, including but not limited to self-report measures, behavioral observations, neurocognitive testing, and psychophysiological indicators. By harnessing the strengths of multiple modalities, clinicians can gain a more comprehensive and holistic perspective on the nature and extent of maladaptive schemas within individuals. For instance, while self-report measures may capture subjective experiences and belief systems, behavioral observations can provide valuable insights into how these schemas manifest in real-life situations, thereby enriching the overall assessment.

On the other hand, integrating multimodal assessments allows for cross-validation and triangulation of data, enhancing the robustness and reliability of the assessment process. By corroborating findings across different modalities, clinicians can mitigate the limitations associated with single-method assessments, thus fostering greater confidence in the diagnostic accuracy and treatment planning. Furthermore, the multidimensionality afforded by multimodal assessments enables the identification of unique patterns and intersections that may otherwise remain unnoticed in unimodal evaluations, paving the way for a more nuanced understanding of schema dynamics.

Beyond the diagnostic utility, the integration of multimodal assessments holds promise for personalized and targeted interventions. By elucidating the diverse dimensions through which maladaptive schemas operate, clinicians can tailor treatment strategies that address the specific manifestations and triggers identified through the integrated assessment process. This individualized approach contributes to the optimization of therapeutic outcomes, as it aligns interventions with the multifaceted nature of schema pathology.

8. Emerging Technologies in Schema Evaluation:

Advancements in technology have significantly influenced the field of schema evaluation, offering innovative approaches to enhance the assessment and understanding of schemas in clinical settings. One prominent emerging technology is virtual reality, a tool that has shown promising potential in capturing and simulating real-life scenarios to assess individuals' cognitive processes and emotional responses. VR-based assessments provide a controlled environment where individuals can confront and interact with situations that trigger their maladaptive schemas, enabling clinicians to observe and analyze their cognitive and emotional reactions in a realistic context. This immersive experience offers valuable insights into the specific triggers and thought patterns associated with various schemas, ultimately aiding in targeted intervention strategies. Additionally, the use of artificial intelligence and machine learning algorithms has opened new avenues for analyzing large datasets to identify patterns and associations related to schema activation and its impact on depressive states. By leveraging AI-powered tools, researchers and clinicians can gain deeper insights into the complex interplay between schemas and depression, leading to more personalized and effective treatment approaches. Moreover, mobile health (mHealth) applications have emerged as practical tools for continuous schema monitoring and self-assessment outside of clinical settings. These user-friendly apps enable individuals to track their mood fluctuations, cognitive distortions, and triggers of maladaptive schemas in real time, providing valuable data for clinicians to better understand their clients' experiences and tailor interventions accordingly. Furthermore, neuroimaging techniques, such as functional magnetic resonance imaging and electroencephalography, have advanced our understanding of the neural correlates of schemas and depression. These technologies allow for the direct observation and measurement of brain activity associated with schema activation, shedding light on the neurological processes underlying depressive symptomatology. Incorporating these neurotechnologies into schema evaluation enhances the objectivity and precision of assessments, facilitating a more comprehensive understanding of the neurobiological underpinnings of maladaptive schemas. As researchers and clinicians continue to explore and integrate these emerging technologies into schema evaluation, ongoing collaboration with technologists and ethical considerations are imperative to ensure the responsible and judicious use of these tools in clinical practice.

# EVIDENCE-BASED STUDIES SUPPORTING COGNITIVE THEORY

## Pioneering Studies and Foundational Evidence

The establishment of cognitive theory in understanding and treating depression was underpinned by a series of pioneering studies that provided foundational evidence for its efficacy. Early investigations, notably led by Aaron Beck and his colleagues, sought to delineate the distinct cognitive processes implicated in the development and maintenance of depressive symptomatology. These seminal studies laid the groundwork for subsequent empirical inquiries and continue to shape contemporary understandings of depression. By systematically examining the cognitive patterns exhibited by individuals with depressive disorders, researchers were able to identify specific thought distortions and dysfunctional beliefs that characterize this condition. The meticulous documentation and analysis of these cognitive phenomena not only validated the theoretical framework proposed by Beck but also set the stage for empirical validation through subsequent research endeavors.

The pioneering studies in this area contributed to the conceptualization of cognitive schemas and their role in shaping an individual's interpretation of experiences and events. Through rigorous experimentation and clinical observation, researchers were able to delineate the cognitive structures that underpin depressive thinking, thus elucidating the interplay between cognition and emotional states. These early investigations also emphasized the need for multifaceted assessment approaches, integrating self-report measures, behavioral observations, and cognitive assessments to comprehensively capture the cognitive landscape of depression. The confluence of these diverse methodological approaches bolstered the credibility of cognitive theory and provided a robust foundation for subsequent research in this domain.

The pioneering studies yielded critical insights into the impact of cognitive interventions on alleviating depressive symptoms. Through meticulously designed experimental protocols, researchers demonstrated the efficacy of cognitive restructuring techniques in ameliorating maladaptive thought patterns and reducing depressive distress. These empirical demonstrations not only affirmed the central tenets of cognitive theory but also paved the way for the development of cognitive-behavioral interventions that have become integral to contemporary therapeutic practices. The depth and breadth of evidence derived from these early studies established a compelling case for the therapeutic potential of addressing cognitive distortions in the treatment of depression, thereby catalyzing a paradigm shift in psychological intervention strategies.

## Longitudinal Analyses of Depressive Symptomatology

Longitudinal analyses of depressive symptomatology provide invaluable insights into the trajectory and persistence of cognitive patterns associated with depression. These studies often span extended durations, capturing the dynamic nature of individuals' experiences with depression over time and shedding light on the complex interplay between cognitive processes and mood disturbances. By longitudinally tracking cognitive phenomena such as self-critical thinking, rumination, and negative schemata, researchers have been able to discern patterns of stability, change, and recurrence in depressive symptomatology. Notably, longitudinal research has elucidated the reciprocal relationship between cognitive patterns and depressive symptoms, underscoring the bidirectional influence wherein cognitive distortions contribute to sustained depressive states, while prolonged depression can reinforce and entrench maladaptive cognitive patterns. Furthermore, longitudinal analyses offer crucial evidence regarding the temporal sequencing of cognitive shifts and mood alterations, enabling a deeper understanding of how cognitive processes predate, co-occur with, and follow periods of depression. These chronologically detailed observations not only inform our comprehension of individual variation in cognitive vulnerabilities but also contribute to refining theoretical models of depression, particularly within the framework of cognitive theory. With a wealth of data amassed through targeted longitudinal investigations, researchers have been able to map nuanced trajectories of cognitive change and persistence across diverse populations, leading to valuable implications for intervention and personalized therapeutic approaches.

## Cross-Cultural Studies and Global Perspectives

Cross-cultural studies provide valuable insights into the manifestation, experience, and interpretation of depressive symptoms across diverse societies and ethnic groups. By comparing and contrasting the prevalence, symptoms, and etiology of depression in different cultural contexts, researchers have identified both commonalities and distinct variations that enrich our understanding of this complex mental health condition.

One fundamental aspect examined in cross-cultural studies is the expression of depressive symptoms. While some manifestations are consistent across cultures, such as feelings of sadness and hopelessness, others may be influenced by cultural norms and values. For example, in individualistic cultures, there may be greater emphasis on personal distress, while in collectivist cultures, interconnectedness and family dynamics may play a more significant role in shaping the expression of depressive symptoms. Understanding these nuances is critical for developing culturally sensitive assessment tools and interventions.

Additionally, cross-cultural studies shed light on the impact of social and environmental factors on the prevalence and course of depression. Socioeconomic disparities, discrimination, acculturation stress, and access to mental health resources can significantly influence the experience and management of depression within different cultural settings. By examining these factors, researchers can identify unique challenges faced by individuals from diverse backgrounds and propose tailored strategies to address disparities in mental health outcomes.

Global perspectives on depression encompass an exploration of cultural beliefs, traditions, and help-seeking behaviors related to mental health. The stigma surrounding mental illness, differing explanatory models of depression, and attitudes towards professional treatment all contribute to the cultural construction of depression. Comparing how various cultures perceive and respond to depression allows for a more nuanced understanding of the complex interplay between sociocultural influences and mental health practices.

**Quantitative Approaches in Evidence Gathering**

By utilizing precise measurement tools and statistical analyses, researchers have been able to quantify the impact of cognitive processes on depressive symptomatology. One key quantitative method is the use of self-report questionnaires such as the Beck Depression Inventory (BDI) and the Hamilton Rating Scale for Depression (HAM-D). These standardized instruments provide an objective assessment of depressive symptoms and allow for comparisons across different populations and treatment interventions.

Experimental designs, including randomized controlled trials (RCTs), have been instrumental in examining the efficacy of cognitive therapy in reducing depressive symptoms. RCTs provide a rigorous framework for testing the effectiveness of cognitive interventions compared to control conditions, establishing causal relationships between the intervention and symptom improvement. Moreover, through the use of outcome measures such as remission rates and reduction in relapse, quantitative data from RCTs offer valuable insights into the long-term impact of cognitive approaches.

In addition, advances in technology have enabled innovative quantitative methodologies in the study of cognitive theory of depression. Neuroimaging techniques, such as functional magnetic resonance imaging and electroencephalography, have allowed researchers to observe the neural correlates of cognitive processes implicated in depression. By quantifying brain activity patterns and mapping neural circuitry, these studies have provided empirical support for the involvement of cognitive mechanisms in the etiology and maintenance of depressive symptoms.

Importantly, meta-analytical reviews have synthesized quantitative data from multiple studies, allowing for a comprehensive overview of the evidence supporting cognitive theory. Meta-analyses aggregate effect sizes across diverse research endeavors, providing a robust statistical examination of the collective findings. Through meta-analytical approaches, researchers have been able to quantify the magnitude of the association between cognitive variables and depression, leading to a better understanding of the overall impact of cognitive factors in the context of depression.

### Qualitative Insights from Patient Case Studies

Qualitative insights obtained from in-depth patient case studies serve as an invaluable source of rich, contextual information that contributes significantly to the validation and refinement of cognitive theory in depression. Through meticulous examination and analysis of individual experiences, emotions, and thought processes, researchers gain access to nuanced understandings that are often obscured by quantitative approaches alone. These insights provide a humanizing dimension to the empirical data, offering glimpses into the lived realities of those grappling with depressive symptoms. Patient narratives unveil the interplay between cognitive patterns, affective states, and behavioral manifestations, shedding light on the deeply personal and subjective nature of depression.

By delving into specific cases, researchers can elucidate the idiosyncratic ways in which cognitive distortions operate within diverse populations, accounting for variations in symptom manifestation and treatment responsiveness. The qualitative exploration of these nuances not only bolsters the theoretical foundation of cognitive theory but also informs the tailoring of therapeutic interventions to better accommodate individual differences and needs. Moreover, it allows for the identification of potential discrepancies or incongruences within the existing tenets of cognitive theory, prompting reevaluation and refinement when warranted.

Patient case studies afford the opportunity to capture the dynamic trajectories of depressive experiences, encompassing the ebbs and flows that characterize the lived reality of individuals over time. Thus, they complement and enrich the snapshot perspectives derived from cross-sectional quantitative analyses, offering longitudinal insights that facilitate a more comprehensive understanding of the complex nature of depression. Through detailed accounts of patients' journeys, researchers can discern the impact of cognitive restructuring, schema-level interventions, and cognitive-behavioral strategies on the reshaping of individuals' outlooks and emotional experiences. This qualitative lens reveals the intricacies underlying therapeutic progress and setbacks, thereby deepening the understanding of the mechanisms through which cognitive theory exerts its influence. It also elucidates the multifaceted nature of resilience and coping strategies employed by individuals in their struggle against depressive cognitive patterns.

### Meta-Analytical Reviews and Their Conclusions

Meta-analytical reviews play a crucial role in synthesizing the vast body of evidence regarding the cognitive theory of depression. Through systematic aggregation and statistical analysis of numerous studies, meta-analyses provide a comprehensive overview of the empirical support for cognitive models of depressive disorders.

Utilizing rigorous methodologies, meta-analytic researchers evaluate the consistency and strength of associations between cognitive variables and depressive symptoms across diverse populations and settings. By examining a broad range of primary studies, meta-analyses facilitate the identification of common patterns, disparities, and potential moderators within the existing literature.

The conclusions drawn from meta-analytic reviews often confirm the substantial impact of cognitive factors on the onset, maintenance, and recurrence of depression. They highlight the robustness of cognitive distortions, maladaptive schemas, and dysfunctional information processing in contributing to the development and exacerbation of depressive symptoms.

Meta-analytic findings shed light on the potential predictive value of cognitive variables in discerning individuals at risk for depressive episodes. By elucidating the magnitude of these associations, meta-analyses offer insights into the relative importance of various cognitive constructs and their differential contributions to the progression of depression.

Additionally, meta-analytic reviews have contributed to addressing conflicting findings and resolving theoretical discrepancies within the cognitive framework. Through subgroup analyses and sensitivity testing, these systematic assessments aid in clarifying when and under what circumstances cognitive theories hold significant explanatory power in understanding depressive psychopathology.

The convergence of findings across different cultural contexts and demographic groups underscores the cross-cutting relevance of cognitive mechanisms in shaping the experience of depression. Meta-analytical syntheses provide compelling evidence supporting the universality of cognitive themes while acknowledging nuances that may arise in specific sociocultural contexts.

**Correlations with Neurobiological Data**

In recent years, there has been a growing interest in understanding the neurobiological underpinnings of cognitive theories of depression, particularly in relation to the prominent work of Aaron Beck. Studies have endeavored to identify neural correlates that may align with the cognitive processes implicated in depressive symptomatology, offering valuable insights into the potential biological foundations of these cognitive phenomena. Advancements in neuroimaging techniques, such as functional magnetic resonance imaging and positron emission tomography, have enabled researchers to explore the neural circuitry associated with cognitive functions relevant to depression. These investigations have revealed intriguing associations between cognitive biases, such as negative interpretation and attentional biases, and alterations in brain regions involved in emotional processing, including the amygdala, prefrontal cortex, and anterior cingulate cortex. Additionally, studies have sought to elucidate the impact of cognition on neuroendocrine function and neurotransmitter systems implicated in mood regulation. The examination of hypothalamic-pituitary-adrenal (HPA) axis dysregulation and abnormalities in serotonin and dopamine signaling has pointed towards potential mechanisms by which cognitive patterns may influence neurobiological pathways linked to depression. Furthermore, research has explored the interplay between genetic factors and cognitive vulnerability, shedding light on gene-environment interactions that could contribute to the development and maintenance of depressive cognitive styles. Integrating findings from neurobiological investigations with cognitive theory provides a platform for a more comprehensive understanding of the multifaceted nature of depression. By uncovering the neural substrates that underpin cognitive processes, clinicians and researchers can potentially refine existing therapeutic approaches and develop novel interventions targeting both cognitive and neurobiological components of depression. This integrated perspective holds promise for advancing personalized treatments and addressing the interplay between cognitive, emotional, and physiological mechanisms in depression.

## Integration with Other Psychological Theories

The integration of cognitive theory with other psychological models represents a rich avenue for enriching our understanding of depression. By bridging concepts and principles across different frameworks, researchers and practitioners can develop more comprehensive and nuanced perspectives on the nature of depressive disorders. One prominent area of integration involves the intersection of cognitive theory with behavioral theories. The merger of cognitive-behavioral approaches has yielded powerful interventions that target both maladaptive thought patterns and unhelpful behavioral cycles. This synergistic blend acknowledges the reciprocal influence between cognition and behavior, paving the way for holistic treatment strategies that address multiple facets of depression.

An exploration of cognitive theory in relation to psychodynamic theories unveils intriguing insights into the interplay of unconscious processes and conscious cognitive structures. This integrative endeavor sheds light on how early experiences and internalized interpersonal dynamics contribute to the development and maintenance of cognitive distortions and negative schemas. Examining depression through this lens underscores the importance of addressing underlying emotional conflicts and relational patterns alongside cognitive restructuring, opening up new dimensions in therapeutic interventions.

The infusion of cognitive theory with humanistic-existential perspectives offers a profound examination of the philosophical and existential dimensions of depression. The existential quandaries surrounding meaning, freedom, and isolation intersect with cognitive processing, shaping individuals' perceptions and interpretations of their experiences. The symbiosis of these two paradigms acknowledges the role of existential angst and the quest for personal authenticity in the manifestation and resolution of depressive symptomatology, prompting a deeper engagement with existential themes in psychotherapeutic work.

Additionally, the convergence of cognitive theory with social ecological frameworks broadens the scope of understanding by elucidating the socio-environmental factors that influence cognitive processes and emotional states. This integration highlights the reciprocal relationships between individual cognition and the larger social context, emphasizing the impact of societal norms, cultural values, and interpersonal dynamics on the development and perpetuation of depressive cognitions. Here, an expanded view of depression emerges, one that encompasses not only intrapersonal dynamics but also contextual influences, calling for multifaceted interventions that address both individual cognitive patterns and environmental stressors.

# CRITIQUES AND COUNTERARGUMENTS OF BECKIAN THEORY

## Analysis of Empirical Limitations

Empirical research forms the cornerstone of scientific inquiry, providing a solid foundation for theories and their practical applications. In the context of critiquing Beck's cognitive theory of depression, it is essential to scrutinize the empirical limitations that arise from the research supporting this framework.

One notable empirical limitation lies in the nature of self-report measures commonly used in assessing cognitive distortions and negative thought patterns. While these instruments provide valuable insight into individuals' subjective experiences, they are inherently susceptible to response biases and may not accurately capture the complexity of cognitive processes in depression. Moreover, reliance on self-report measures poses challenges in generalizing findings across diverse populations and cultural contexts, highlighting the need for more robust and culturally sensitive assessment tools.

Another crucial aspect pertains to the overreliance on correlational studies in elucidating the relationship between cognitive processes and depressive symptoms. Correlational designs, while informative, do not establish causal relationships between cognitive factors and depression, thereby limiting the capacity to infer direct implications for therapeutic interventions. Longitudinal studies and experimental designs are imperative to discern the temporal and causal dynamics underlying cognitive processes in depression, presenting a critical area for methodological refinement.

The majority of empirical studies underpinning Beck's theory have predominantly focused on outpatient samples with mild to moderate depressive symptoms, raising questions about the generalizability of findings to individuals with severe or treatment-resistant depression. This bias in sampling poses challenges in fully understanding the applicability of cognitive theory across the spectrum of depressive disorders, prompting the need for inclusive research that encompasses diverse clinical presentations.

The dearth of neurobiological markers and objective measures linked to cognitive processes in depression presents a significant empirical challenge. While cognitive theories emphasize the interplay between thoughts, emotions, and behaviors, integrating neurobiological data is imperative to gain a comprehensive understanding of the underlying mechanisms. The limited integration of neuroscientific approaches in validating cognitive constructs underscores the necessity for interdisciplinary collaborations to bridge this empirical gap.

**Conceptual Challenges and Alternative Theories**

As practitioners continue to delve into the intricacies of depressive symptomatology, various challenges and alternative perspectives have emerged that warrant thoughtful consideration. One notable challenge relates to the question of whether cognitive distortions represent the primary causal factor of depression or if they are symptomatic of deeper underlying processes. Critics argue that while cognitive distortions may contribute to the maintenance of depressive states, they may not necessarily be the root cause. This raises fundamental questions about the directionality of the relationship between cognition and mood, directing attention to broader etiological frameworks.

In exploring alternative theories, researchers have examined the interplay of biological, environmental, and sociocultural factors in shaping individuals' experiences of depression. The diathesis-stress model, for instance, posits that certain predispositions interact with external stressors, leading to the onset of depressive symptoms. This theoretical framework broadens the scope beyond cognitive processes, emphasizing the multifaceted nature of psychological disorders.

The psychodynamic perspective offers an alternative lens through which to understand depressive phenomena. Proponents of this viewpoint underscore the significance of unconscious conflicts, early life experiences, and interpersonal dynamics in influencing an individual's emotional well-being. This approach challenges the exclusive emphasis on surface-level cognitive content, urging scholars to explore subconscious mechanisms and relational patterns that may underpin depressive manifestations.

Recent advancements in neuroscience have invigorated discussions surrounding the neurobiological underpinnings of depression. Research has elucidated the complex interconnections between neural circuitry, neurotransmitter function, and affective regulation, casting light on potential neural correlates of depressive symptomatology. This neurobiological perspective invites a nuanced exploration of the biological determinants of mental illness, providing a complementary framework to cognitive theories.

## Role of Cultural Factors in Cognitive Theory

Understanding how cultural elements intersect with cognitive theory is essential for providing effective and culturally sensitive interventions for individuals from diverse backgrounds. It is imperative to acknowledge that cognition itself is influenced by cultural norms, values, beliefs, and societal expectations.

One of the primary considerations in the cultural lens is the impact of collectivism versus individualism. Cultures that prioritize collectivism, where community and interconnectedness are paramount, may perceive and express depressive symptoms differently than cultures that emphasize individualism. For example, individuals from collectivist cultures may be more inclined to describe their depressive experiences in relational terms, such as feeling like a burden on their family or failing to meet communal expectations, while those from individualistic cultures may focus more on personal achievement or autonomy as sources of distress.

Cultural differences can influence the interpretation and experience of cognitive distortions. For instance, certain cognitive distortions identified in Beck's theory, such as personalization or arbitrary inference, may manifest differently based on cultural contexts. Similarly, the content and themes of maladaptive schemas may vary across cultures, reflecting the specific societal, familial, and interpersonal dynamics prevalent in each cultural milieu.

Another crucial aspect is the role of stigma and help-seeking behaviors. Cultural attitudes towards mental health, stigma associated with psychological distress, and perceptions of seeking professional help significantly impact the recognition and management of depressive symptoms. In some cultures, seeking mental health support may be stigmatized or viewed as a sign of weakness, leading individuals to underreport or attribute their symptoms to physical ailments. Such cultural nuances have implications for the identification and treatment of depression within the cognitive paradigm.

Additionally, language and expression styles can shape the communication of depressive experiences. Translating cognitive therapy techniques and concepts into different languages and adapting them to resonate with diverse linguistic and cultural nuances is a critical consideration for effective implementation. Furthermore, cultural competency and humility among practitioners are vital for establishing rapport and fostering trust with clients from various cultural backgrounds.

### Critiques from the Neurobiological Framework

The examination of Beck's Cognitive Theory through the lens of the neurobiological framework provides a comprehensive understanding of its limitations and challenges. Within this critique, the focus is on unraveling how the biological underpinnings of depression intersect with the cognitive model, shedding light on the complex interplay between genetic, neural, and environmental factors. While cognitive theory emphasizes the centrality of dysfunctional thinking patterns in the etiology and maintenance of depression, neurobiological critiques interrogate the oversights in neglecting the workings of the brain and its impact on affective processes.

A critical aspect lies in the mechanisms of neurotransmitters and their perturbations in mood disorders. The serotonin hypothesis, for instance, has been extensively studied in the context of depression, raising questions about the oversimplification of attributing depressive symptoms solely to cognitive distortions while overlooking the role of neurotransmitter dysregulation. Additionally, neuroimaging studies have unveiled alterations in brain structures, such as the prefrontal cortex and amygdala, which are integral to emotional regulation and cognitive processing. These findings warrant an exploration of how these neural aberrations interact with cognitive patterns, challenging the narrow focus of cognitive theory.

Proponents of the neurobiological critique argue for a more nuanced perspective that encompasses the bidirectional influence of biology and cognition. While acknowledging the significance of cognitive schemas in shaping one's interpretation of experiences, the neurobiological framework advocates for the incorporation of neural mechanisms in modulating these cognitive processes. The entwined nature of biological predispositions and cognitive appraisals underscores the need for a holistic understanding that transcends the exclusive emphasis on thoughts and beliefs.

The burgeoning field of epigenetics introduces a new dimension to the critique, highlighting the intergenerational transmission of stress-related vulnerabilities that remain unaddressed within the confines of cognitive theory. This calls for an expanded scope that encompasses the heritability of epigenetic modifications and their potential impact on cognitive-affective patterns. Such a broadened perspective not only enriches our comprehension of depression but also cautions against overlooking the intricacies of gene-environment interactions in shaping individual vulnerabilities to depressive symptomatology.

## Divergences in Global Application

Cognitive Theory of Depression's applicability across diverse cultural contexts has generated considerable debate and critical scrutiny within the field of psychology. The globalization of psychological theories poses an inherent challenge due to variations in cultural norms, values, and expressions of distress.

One of the prominent concerns pertains to the cross-cultural validity of cognitive distortions and schemas postulated in Beck's theory. While empirical evidence largely stems from Western populations, the transposition of these constructs onto non-Western societies raises pertinent questions about the extent to which they reflect the nuances of depressive experiences across different cultural landscapes. This necessitates a reevaluation of the theoretical underpinnings, particularly regarding the universality of cognitive processes implicated in depression.

The varying cultural perceptions of help-seeking behaviors and mental health stigmatization compound the challenges in the global application of cognitive interventions for depression. The acceptance and efficacy of cognitive therapy may differ significantly across cultures, underscoring the need for culturally sensitive modifications to therapeutic approaches. This calls for a more inclusive examination of the sociocultural determinants of depression and corresponding adaptations in the delivery of cognitive interventions.

The divergence in global application is also manifested in the translation and adaptation of cognitive therapy protocols. Language nuances and idiomatic expressions present formidable obstacles in ensuring accurate and faithful transference of therapeutic content. Cultural idioms of distress and localized conceptualizations of emotions further engender complexities in effectively disseminating and implementing cognitive strategies for depression.

Beyond linguistic considerations, the socioecological contexts in which individuals experience depression greatly influence the utility and relevance of cognitive interventions. Socioeconomic disparities, political climates, and access to mental health resources profoundly shape the manifestation and management of depression. Accordingly, the global dissemination of cognitive theory necessitates contextual congruity to address the intersecting layers of cultural, social, and economic influences on depression.

## Reexamination of Cognitions in Severe Depression

Severe depression presents a complex landscape for the cognitive theory approach. In severe cases, the traditional understanding of cognitive distortions and dysfunctional beliefs may not fully capture the depth and breadth of the individual's internal experiences.

When confronting severe depression, individuals often experience an overwhelming sense of hopelessness, profound self-loathing, and debilitating despair. In exploring their cognitions, it becomes evident that their thought patterns encompass a pervasive and enduring negative outlook on life, themselves, and the future. However, the traditional cognitive model may fall short in encapsulating the intense and pervasive nature of these negative cognitions in severe depression.

Individuals with severe depression frequently exhibit cognitive patterns that involve extreme and rigid thinking, marked by a heightened sensitivity to perceived failures or rejections. These cognitive characteristics may manifest in forms such as rumination, relentless self-blame, and overwhelming guilt, fueling the cycle of despair and exacerbating the severity of the condition. By reexamining these cognitive processes, we aim to deepen our understanding of the interplay between cognition and emotional distress in severe depression.

It is crucial to acknowledge that individuals experiencing severe depression often struggle with cognitive impairments that extend beyond maladaptive thinking patterns. Cognitive deficits, including difficulties in concentration, memory disturbances, and executive functioning challenges, significantly impact daily functioning and exacerbate the individual's sense of helplessness and worthlessness. These cognitive impairments contribute to the complexity of severe depression, necessitating a comprehensive reexamination of cognitions within this context.

**Synthesis of Psychological and Biological Integrations**

In the sphere of cognitive theory and its application to depression, a growing body of research has underscored the necessity of synthesizing psychological and biological perspectives. This amalgamation seeks to forge a more comprehensive understanding of depressive phenomena, encompassing not only cognitive processes but also their interplay with neurobiological underpinnings. At the core of this pursuit lies the recognition that the mind and body are inextricably linked, impacting one another in multifaceted ways.

An exploration of psychological and biological integrations necessitates an interdisciplinary approach, drawing from fields such as neuroscience, psychology, psychiatry, and psychobiology. In dissecting the complexities of depression, it becomes apparent that cognitive mechanisms do not operate in isolation; rather, they intersect with neural pathways, biochemical imbalances, and genetic predispositions. Examining these intersections unlocks valuable insights into the etiology, progression, and treatment of depressive disorders, shedding light on the nuanced interdependencies between cognition and biology.

While cognitive theory has traditionally emphasized the role of maladaptive thought patterns in shaping depressive experiences, an integrated framework expands this lens to encompass the network of neurotransmitter dysregulation, neuroplasticity, and structural brain changes that accompany depression. Moreover, it acknowledges the bidirectional nature of psychological and biological factors—how cognition can influence neurobiology, and conversely, how neurobiological processes can impact cognitive functioning and emotional regulation. This interplay underscores the indispensability of melding psychological and biological dimensions in elucidating the complexity of depression.

To operationalize this synthesis, researchers have utilized advanced neuroimaging techniques, such as functional magnetic resonance imaging and positron emission tomography, to investigate the neural correlates of cognitive processes implicated in depression. These studies have unraveled the neural substrates of cognitive distortions, rumination, and negative schema activation, providing empirical substantiation for the connection between cognition and brain function in depressive states. Concurrently, genetic studies have delved into the heritability of cognitive vulnerabilities and their interaction with genetic markers related to mood disorders, unveiling the interweaving of genetic predispositions and cognitive-affective dynamics.

The advancement of psychoneuroimmunology has further illuminated the interconnectedness of psychological, neurological, and immunological facets in depression. Research in this domain has illuminated the reciprocal influence between stress-related cognitive patterns and immune dysregulation, amplifying our comprehension of the systemic ramifications of depression. Such advancements culminate in a holistic rendering of depression, transcending reductionist viewpoints by integrating the tapestry of cognitive, neurological, and physiological components. Through this synthesis, novel avenues for therapeutic interventions emerge, harnessing the unity of psychological and biological insights to devise targeted treatments that concomitantly address cognitive distortions and underlying neurobiological aberrations.

## FUTURE DIRECTIONS AND RESEARCH OPPORTUNITIES

### Gaps in Current Research

Research in the field of cognitive approaches to depression has made significant progress in understanding the underlying mechanisms and treatment strategies. However, as we look towards the future, it is crucial to acknowledge and address the existing gaps in current research. One prominent gap lies in the need for more comprehensive longitudinal studies that track the long-term efficacy of cognitive interventions. While numerous short-term studies have demonstrated the benefits of cognitive therapy, there is a paucity of research examining its sustained impact over extended periods, posing a critical gap in knowledge. Moreover, the majority of existing studies have been conducted in clinical settings, warranting the exploration of real-world applications and effectiveness outside controlled environments. Another pertinent gap pertains to the intersection of cognitive theory with diverse cultural contexts. The bulk of research has been conducted in Western populations, limiting the generalizability of findings across different ethnic and cultural groups. Understanding how cognitive approaches manifest in varied cultural settings and tailoring interventions accordingly is essential for global relevance and efficacy. Additionally, there is a need for further investigation into the potential integration of cognitive techniques with emerging technologies such as virtual reality and artificial intelligence. While initial studies have shown promise, there remains a gap in understanding the optimal ways to synergize traditional cognitive frameworks with innovative technology. Furthermore, exploring the role of neuroplasticity and its implications for refining cognitive interventions represents an exciting yet underexplored avenue.

### Innovative Methodologies for Advancing Cognitive Theory

The advancement of cognitive theory necessitates the exploration of innovative methodologies that can push the boundaries of traditional frameworks and propel the field forward. One promising avenue for advancing cognitive theory lies in the integration of neuroimaging techniques, such as functional magnetic resonance imaging and electroencephalography, to deepen our understanding of the neural underpinnings of cognitive processes in depression. By leveraging these technologies, researchers can delve into the workings of the brain and unravel the specific neural circuitries implicated in cognitive distortions and maladaptive schema, shedding light on the underlying mechanisms of depressive symptomatology.

On the other hand, the utilization of advanced statistical modeling and machine learning algorithms holds immense potential for mining large datasets and identifying complex patterns within cognitive processes that may have previously eluded detection. These modern computational approaches can aid in uncovering subtle nuances and correlations, providing a more nuanced and comprehensive comprehension of cognitive functioning in depression. Additionally, the integration of virtual reality technology presents a novel opportunity to simulate real-life scenarios and induce cognitive challenges in a controlled setting, offering a unique platform for exploring cognitive biases and schemas within an immersive environment.

Another innovative methodology involves the incorporation of ecological momentary assessment (EMA) and ambulatory monitoring through smartphone applications, wearable devices, and ecological momentary interventions (EMIs). This approach enables real-time tracking of individuals' cognitive processes and emotional states within their natural environments, allowing for a dynamic and ecologically valid assessment of cognitive patterns and maladaptive thought processes as they unfold in daily life. It also paves the way for personalized interventions that can be tailored based on individual cognitive profiles and fluctuations in mood.

The burgeoning field of computational psychiatry offers a rich source of innovative methodologies, integrating principles from computer science, mathematics, and neuroscience to construct computational models that elucidate the underlying mechanisms governing cognitive dysfunction in depression. These models can not only provide insights into the etiology of cognitive disturbances but also offer a framework for devising targeted interventions that address specific cognitive deficits.

### The Integration of Technology into Traditional Cognitive Frameworks

In the rapidly evolving landscape of mental health interventions, the convergence of technology and traditional cognitive frameworks stands as a pivotal point of interest. The integration of technology into established therapeutic modalities holds the promise of enhancing accessibility, personalization, and efficacy of treatments for individuals experiencing depression and other psychological conditions. From the application of virtual reality to simulate real-life scenarios for exposure therapy to the development of mobile applications that facilitate ongoing monitoring and self-management, technological advancements have expanded the possibilities within cognitive approaches.

One notable avenue of exploration lies in the sphere of artificial intelligence and machine learning. AI algorithms can analyze large datasets to identify patterns and predict individual responses to specific cognitive interventions. This not only enables clinicians to tailor treatment plans according to the needs and preferences of each patient but also offers insights into refining existing cognitive models. Furthermore, the emergence of telehealth platforms has redefined the delivery of cognitive therapy, allowing individuals to access evidence-based interventions remotely, thereby dismantling geographical barriers and addressing disparities in mental health care accessibility. Consequently, this marriage of technology and cognitive frameworks has the potential to extend the reach of effective interventions to underserved populations.

On the other hand, the advent of wearable devices and sensor technologies presents opportunities for real-time monitoring of physiological and behavioral indicators. By integrating such data streams with cognitive assessments, practitioners can garner a comprehensive understanding of an individual's experiences and progress, thus forming the basis for more nuanced and adaptive interventions. Additionally, the utilization of biofeedback mechanisms provides clients with tangible representations of their psychological states, fostering increased self-awareness and active engagement in therapeutic processes.

Nevertheless, the integration of technology with traditional cognitive frameworks necessitates careful consideration of ethical, privacy, and security concerns. Ensuring the protection of sensitive information, maintaining user autonomy, and safeguarding against potential misuse of personal data are essential prerequisites to harnessing the full potential of technological innovations within mental health contexts. As such, collaborative endeavors between technologists, mental health professionals, and ethicists become imperative in charting the future trajectory of this amalgamation.

### Interdisciplinary Collaborations and Their Potential Impact

Interdisciplinary collaborations have become increasingly important in the field of cognitive-based therapy as researchers and practitioners recognize the value of integrating insights from diverse disciplines. By fostering partnerships between psychologists, neuroscientists, sociologists, and other relevant experts, a more comprehensive understanding of depression and cognitive approaches can be achieved. These collaborations can lead to innovative research methodologies that combine cognitive theories with empirical data from fields such as neurobiology, sociology, and anthropology. The potential impact of these collaborations is significant, as they can enhance the effectiveness of cognitive-based therapy by incorporating a broader range of perspectives and insights. In addition, interdisciplinary collaborations can contribute to the development of more holistic and personalized treatment approaches, taking into account the complex interplay between cognitive processes, social factors, and biological mechanisms. Furthermore, such collaborations can facilitate the translation of research findings into practical applications, leading to the development of more targeted and effective interventions for individuals struggling with depression. Through interdisciplinary collaborations, cognitive approaches can also benefit from advancements in related fields, such as artificial intelligence and digital health technologies. This cross-pollination of ideas and techniques has the potential to revolutionize the delivery of cognitive-based therapy, making it more accessible, adaptable, and responsive to individual needs. Moreover, interdisciplinary collaborations can address cultural and societal factors that influence the experience and expression of depression, allowing for the development of culturally sensitive and contextually relevant therapeutic strategies. By engaging in interdisciplinary collaborations, the field of cognitive-based therapy can continue to evolve and stay at the forefront of innovation, ultimately benefiting individuals worldwide who are affected by depression.

### Emergent Themes in Cognitive-Based Therapy

The landscape of cognitive-based therapy is continuously evolving, giving rise to emergent themes that shape the future of psychological treatment. One notable emergent theme is the integration of mindfulness techniques within cognitive therapy. The synergy between mindfulness and cognitive restructuring has garnered significant attention in recent years, with robust evidence supporting its efficacy in alleviating various mental health concerns, including depression and anxiety. Moreover, the incorporation of positive psychology principles into cognitive interventions represents a forward-looking trend. By accentuating strengths, resilience, and well-being, practitioners are poised to foster holistic healing and transformative growth in their clients. Another pivotal aspect pertains to the personalized application of cognitive strategies. Tailoring interventions to individual differences, such as personality traits, cultural backgrounds, and contextual factors, underscores the adaptability and inclusivity of cognitive therapy. Furthermore, the intersection of neuroscience and cognitive psychology unfolds as a compelling frontier. Advancements in neuroimaging and psychophysiology offer unprecedented insights into the underlying mechanisms of cognitive processes, enriching our understanding of mental health conditions and refining targeted treatments. Additionally, the burgeoning role of technology in cognitive interventions cannot be overlooked. Virtual reality exposure therapy, smartphone applications for mood monitoring, and teletherapy platforms demonstrate the innovative convergence of digital tools with traditional cognitive frameworks, enhancing accessibility and engagement for diverse populations. As the field expands, ethical considerations surrounding the use of technology necessitate careful deliberation. Finally, the shift towards transdiagnostic approaches signals a paradigmatic shift in cognitive therapy. Recognizing overlapping symptomatology across disorders, transdiagnostic interventions provide a unified framework for addressing common cognitive patterns and emotional regulation difficulties. This inclusive and streamlined approach has the potential to optimize resource allocation and treatment efficiency, heralding a new era in evidence-based practice. The emergent themes elucidated here underscore the dynamism inherent in cognitive-based therapy and foreshadow a future characterized by innovation, versatility, and human-centered care.

### Challenges and Ethical Considerations in Future Research

One of the foremost challenges in conducting future research in the sphere of cognitive approaches is the need to address complex ethical considerations. As the field continues to evolve, researchers must remain vigilant in upholding ethical standards to ensure the safety and well-being of study participants. Issues such as informed consent, confidentiality, and potential psychological distress must be conscientiously addressed throughout the research process. Additionally, the cultural sensitivity of cognitive techniques and interventions poses a significant ethical consideration. Ensuring that these approaches are applicable and respectful across diverse cultural contexts is imperative to maintain ethical integrity. Another crucial challenge lies in the responsible use of technology in research. With the advancement of artificial intelligence and digital platforms, researchers face ethical dilemmas regarding data security, privacy, and the potential for biases in technology-driven cognitive assessments. The ethical implications of using technology to deliver cognitive interventions also require careful deliberation, particularly concerning accessibility and equity. Furthermore, researchers must grapple with the ethical ramifications of disseminating their findings. Upholding the principles of transparency, accuracy, and impartiality in the communication of research outcomes is essential for maintaining the integrity of the field. Addressing commercial interests and conflicts of interest presents an ongoing challenge, requiring deliberate efforts to uphold research ethics. Moreover, as cognitive approaches expand globally, ethical considerations related to cross-border collaborations, intellectual property rights, and resource distribution emerge as complex issues. Balancing the pursuit of knowledge with ethical responsibilities demands a nuanced approach to managing these challenges. Ultimately, confronting these ethical and moral quandaries in future research is fundamental to fostering a trustworthy and socially responsible landscape within cognitive approaches.

## 50 STATEMENTS ON BECKIAN THEORY OF DEPRESSION

### On Negative Self-Schema

Depressed individuals interpret experiences through a self-critical lens.

They habitually view themselves as inadequate or unworthy.

Self-evaluations are dominated by feelings of failure.

People with depression often expect rejection or disappointment.

Their self-schema filters out positive feedback.

### On the Cognitive Triad

The depressed person tends to see themselves negatively.

They expect the world to be unsupportive or punishing.

They believe the future holds little promise.

This triad reinforces feelings of hopelessness.

Shifts in any element of the triad can alter mood.

### On Automatic Thoughts

Spontaneous negative thoughts arise without conscious intent.

These thoughts are accepted as facts by the depressed individual.

Automatic thoughts often magnify failure and minimize success.

They occur in response to everyday events.

Becoming aware of these thoughts is central to change.

**On Cognitive Distortions**

Overgeneralizing from a single negative event.

Viewing situations in black-and-white terms.

Exaggerating the likelihood of adverse outcomes.

Discounting positive occurrences as flukes.

Personalizing neutral events as personal failures.

**On Negative Beliefs and Assumptions**

Depressed individuals hold rules about how they should perform or be treated.

Beliefs such as “I must not make mistakes” increase distress.

Core beliefs about unlovability feed depression.

Assumptions about control and self-worth maintain negative mood.

Challenging these beliefs is key to recovery.

**On Hopelessness and Future Outlook**

A bleak view of the future predicts severity of depression.

Expecting continued difficulty undermines motivation.

Hopelessness intensifies negative self-evaluation.

Belief that change is unlikely deepens depressive symptoms.

Altering future expectations can reduce depressive thinking.

**On the Relationship Between Thought and Mood**

How a person interprets events determines emotional response.

Changing thought patterns can change feelings.

Thoughts are the immediate determinants of mood.

Unhelpful thinking fuels emotional pain.

Cognitive restructuring alleviates depressive affect.

**On Behavioral Consequences of Cognition**

Negative thinking leads to withdrawal and inactivity.

Low engagement with rewarding activities sustains depression.

Cognitive change often precedes behavioral change.

Behavior reinforces cognitive patterns.

Increasing engaged behavior supports cognitive change.

**On Therapy and Change Processes**

Therapy helps identify and test negative beliefs.

Collaborative empiricism fosters discovery of alternative views.

Self-monitoring increases awareness of thought patterns.

Behavioral experiments test accuracy of beliefs.

Cognitive change leads to symptom relief.

**On Resilience and Relapse Prevention**

Recognizing early signs of negative thinking prevents relapse.

Sustained cognitive skills support long-term mood regulation.

Adaptive thinking fosters resilience.

Awareness of triggers helps maintain progress.

Cognitive tools generalize beyond therapy sessions.

www.ingramcontent.com/pod-product-compliance
Lightning Source LLC
LaVergne TN
LVHW052316200926
848481LV00002B/583